THE JOSHUA PRIEST

A Biography of Faith

THE JOSHUA PRIEST

A Biography of Faith

BARBARA BENJAMIN

Nepperhan Press
Yonkers, NY

2010
Nepperhan Press, LLC
Yonkers, NY 10702

First Edition

Printed in the United States of America

Library of Congress Control Number: 2010922484
ISBN: 978-0-9794579-7-5

COVER PHOTOGRAPH
Sunrise at Tide Mill Farm, Edmunds, ME
by Barbara Benjamin

Dedicated to our Holy Mother who answered "Yes"

Acknowledgments

The writing of this book took place over a period of twenty-five years, during which time the role of living faith in the ministry of Father Joseph Francis Girzone, The Joshua Priest, became increasingly evident to me. While his Joshua books were inspiring millions of readers worldwide, I found myself being even more inspired by the faith that informed and shaped the life of the author.

I am most grateful to Father Joe for allowing me to share the story of the deeply rooted faith that I have witnessed, and continue to witness, working in his life. Hopefully, this story will inspire others to acknowledge the power of faith in their lives and experience the courage and transformation that such faith engenders.

I also extend my heartfelt thanks to Father Philippe Charles who read the manuscript and encouraged my efforts; to Marie Milton whose expert proofreading provided precision and eloquence to the final draft; and to Karen Weinstein whose cover and book design brought visual beauty and form to my words.

I am grateful, above all, to a loving and humble God who directs my path and makes all things possible.

Contents

Foreword

~

My first encounter with Father Joseph Francis Girzone had all the earmarks of an invitation to destiny. Father Joe had just finished self publishing the first edition of *Joshua* and was making the rounds, as it were, introducing the main character, Joshua, to just about anyone who would listen. On this particular early spring afternoon in 1987, he had been invited to the home of my neighbors, Helene and Ed Rothenbucher, to speak to a handful of their family and friends.

I had called Helene earlier that day about some now forgotten detail of daily life, and, just before she hung up, obviously as a second thought, she somewhat tentatively invited me to join her gathering. Some weeks before, she had given me a copy of *Joshua* to read, but, at the time of Father Joe's visit, I had not yet opened the book. Not letting that stop me, I happily accepted her invitation and, some hours later, walked the half mile or so down the quiet country lane to her house. A promise of renewal filled the air in the sun-bathed April woodland. I knocked at the door, greeted my neighbors, petted their dog, and shook hands with Father Joe.

Dressed in a short-sleeved, plaid, open-necked cotton shirt and tan slacks, he looked no more like a Roman Catholic priest than anyone else in the room. I was immediately intrigued. On

i

the one hand, he had a distinctively deep, calm, accepting spirit that radiated a rare mixture of conviction and humility and evoked unquestioning trust. On the other hand, he presented himself as just an ordinary man, without any outward sign of his vocation. He was different from any clergyman I had ever met; and as the afternoon wore on, I was becoming more and more curious about this encounter.

By the time we finished lunch and Father Joe had introduced us all to Joshua, my curiosity was giving way to an overwhelming certainty: I became certain that I had been touched in a way that would forever change my life as I had known it. I had no clear image of what that change would be or how it would come about, but I had a strong sense that God's hand was present in the events of that day.

Still somewhat mystified, I was not in the least prepared for Father Joe's parting words to me. Making his way toward the front door, shaking hands, and preparing to leave, Father Joe stopped for a moment, smiled at me, and observed: "You have a very special personal relationship with God. It shows in the way you speak, in your tone of voice, even in the way you walk."

I most definitely had never been conscious of any such relationship, and I thought his observation was absurd. Confused by his remarks, I snapped back: "You're a priest – you're the one with the personal relationship with God, not me."

"No," Father Joe insisted, with a composed, concise, and uncompromising conviction that I would come to treasure: "I have other gifts! Your gift is your personal relationship with God."

Perhaps sensing my deep attraction to his Joshua message and, perhaps, also sensing my reservations, Father Joe had, with his parting words, effectively reinforced my impression that this was a day I would never forget.

In the days and years to come, Father Joe would touch millions of lives with his deep faith, his deep love for Jesus, and his timely and powerful Joshua stories; and I would come to discern the essence of the gift that I had received in meeting him that afternoon.

I would also come to understand the gift he saw in me and the nature of his distinct gifts. I would come to understand the integrity of his *fiat*, his innate and unconditional faith, his unwavering obedience, his seasoned humility, and his fearless commitment to Jesus and to Christian unity. Above all, I would come to realize that on that bright April afternoon, I had met The Joshua Priest.

As our friendship grew through the years, and as I grew in the understanding of his spiritual teachings, I became increasingly interested in the singular nature of The Joshua Priest. At the same time, the Joshua books began to have a life of their own and followed one after another onto best-seller lists and into reprint after reprint in one language and then another. Father Joe's speaking tours and retreats began demanding all his time and energy, and so he often found himself having to write on the run. In five short years, Joshua became universally recognized as a friend to people of all religions and nationalities, renewing their hope, their joy, and their faith. Joshua found his way into the Vatican and into the hearts of Jews, Muslims, Hindus, Buddhists, and every denomination of Christians alike.

Through it all, Father Joe remained focused on his most cherished dream: to introduce the world to the loving and caring Jesus who was his constant companion through life. Like a solicitous parent protecting his child, Father Joe protected this dream from any detractors who might not comprehend and, therefore, feared the impact of his clear and powerful stories. He dedicated himself totally to Joshua and to the healing that people found in Joshua. More fully than he had ever imagined possible, he came to realize this dream, and this dream became his ministry. As he traveled the world introducing people to Joshua, he became The Joshua Priest, defining a renewed path of devotion for himself and for all those who respond to God's call to service.

In the process, Father Joe continued to discover a deepening well of physical and spiritual strength that he could draw upon in carrying out his unique ministry. In the twenty-five years since I met him, while most of the world came to know Father Joe as the messenger whose gifts of writing and speaking helped him spread the "good news" of our Savior's unconditional love for us, I came to know Father Joe as a man gifted with extraordinary faith, a living faith that was the foundation for his daily acts of courage and commitment.

What follows on these pages is a biography of that faith, a faith that shaped the life of one of God's most profound contemporary messengers. Set against the background of a world in the midst of political, economic, and scientific upheaval, not unlike our own times, this biography is a testimony to God's timeless and steadfast love and His glorious plan for each of us. It is a story that reveals, by striking examples, the power of living faith.

THE JOSHUA PRIEST

A Biography of Faith

Chapter One

~

Living Faith

I do believe, help my unbelief.
(Mark 9:24)

This is the story of a man, the story of a priest, and the story of faith, as if faith has a life of its own - and it does! We need only examine the growth of faith in our lives or in the lives of people we know to see faith's distinct and powerful existence, a living force that shapes perceptions, personalities, and behavior. While not everyone we know lives a life of faith, those who do have a special presence. We can identify them by their strong, gentle manner, their underlying calmness, their personal sense of freedom and courage, their unwavering optimism, and, above all, their bright, clear, happy eyes. We all have lives in which we grow. Some of us grow wise; others simply grow old. Faith, on the other hand, never grows old; and a life of faith always leads to wisdom. It is the living force of faith that makes the existence of God transparent in everything we see and in everything we do, in the gifts of joy and peace we receive in good times and in the mercy and strength we receive in difficult times.

This living faith is a gift of God, a gift offered openly and freely to everyone, but, like all God's gifts, the gift of faith is not always openly received, even by people who yearn to receive it. The poignancy of this unrequited yearning is so well expressed to Jesus by the father of the epileptic boy: "I do believe, help my unbelief" (Mark 9:24), he cries out, desperately seeking the faith he needs to believe that Jesus can heal his son. As much as we may want to believe, to receive God's gift of living faith, we often are, like the father of the epileptic boy, burdened by "unbelief."

In her book, *A Rocking Horse Catholic,* Caryll Houselander explains how the ability to receive the gift of faith can be damaged in earliest childhood:

> Emotionally children identify their parents with God. They stand for the things that the idea of God stands for to the human race as a whole – security, home, refuge, food and warmth and light, things taken for granted as unquestioningly as the love which provides them is taken for granted, and with the same innocent egoism of childhood. On the day that a young child learns that his trust in father and mother was misplaced, above all if one or the other has sacrificed him to some other love, emotionally if not consciously his trust in God is shattered. He will not, of course, reflect that circumstances may have overcome his parents; he looked to them for the invulnerability, the unchanging love that belongs only to God.[1]

Unconditional faith is bound to our unconditional trust in

a loving and powerful God. Our behavior and actions throughout our lives reflect the strength of our faith, and these actions are the outward proof of the extent to which we trust God. If that trust has been damaged by life experiences, we struggle with the burden of "unbelief." If, on the other hand, we have been able to sustain an unconditional, childlike trust in God, we experience the force of living faith in our lives. In the face of all earthly distractions and discouragements, we are able to see and to trust God's hand guiding our lives and inspiring our actions. The word "faith," itself, has its root in the Indo-European word, *bheidh*, which translated means trust.[2]

For some whose trust in God has been damaged, faith is a constant struggle with "unbelief"; for others whose trust has been severely damaged, it may even be unreachable. For a rare few, however, this faith is egosyntonic, so much a part of them that they don't even notice it is there, except on the rare occasions when that faith is tested. Such people offer themselves to God daily, to be of service to Him, and to fulfill His divine purpose in their lives; and they are aware of God's presence in all they experience.

Throughout the Old Testament and the Gospels, we see examples of those whose faith is egosyntonic and of those who struggle with "unbelief." Abraham, who became the father of the Israelites and, in millennia after, the patriarch of all Christians and Muslims, displayed unconditional trust in God, even to the point of obeying God's request to take his only son, Isaac, up Mount Moriah to kill him with his own hand. His unconditional trust became the model upon which all Abrahamic religions were built. St. Paul explains why Abraham is "the father of all of us" (Romans 4:16): "It was not through the law that the promise was made to

Abraham and his descendants that he would inherit the world, but through the righteousness that comes from faith" (Romans 4:13).

Moses, on the other hand, struggled with "unbelief." So great was his "unbelief" that he disobeyed God. In the desert, with the Israelites and their animals thirsting for water, God instructs Moses: "Take the staff and assemble the community, you and your brother Aaron, and in their presence order the rock to yield its waters. From the rock you shall bring forth water for the community and their livestock to drink" (Numbers 20:8). Moses, struggling with "unbelief," disobeys God, taking credit for the action when he addresses the community: "Listen to me, you rebels! Are we to bring water for you out of this rock" (Numbers 20:10). Moses then strikes the rock twice with his staff, "…and water gushed out in abundance" (Numbers 20:11). As a consequence of his behavior, Moses was denied entrance into the Promised Land: "But the Lord said to Moses and Aaron, 'Because you were not faithful to me in showing forth my sanctity before the Israelites, you shall not lead this community into the land I will give them.'" (Numbers 20:12).

In the Garden at Gethsemane, we see more clearly than anywhere else in the Bible the anatomy of living faith. Here, facing crucifixion, Jesus struggles with trust and, ultimately, proclaims his unconditional faith. He prays: "My Father, if it is possible, let this cup pass from me, yet not as I will but as you will" (Matthew 26:39). Unresolved, he prays again: "The spirit is willing, but the flesh is weak….My Father, if it is not possible that this cup pass without my drinking it, your will be done!" (Matthew 26:41-42). Finally, praying a third time, "…saying the same thing again" (Matthew 26:44), Jesus is resolved, with unconditional trust and faith, to do his Father's will. We can see in Jesus' agony in Gethsemane that unconditional trust and faith include struggling: "The flesh is weak," and we are all human.

Again on the Cross, Jesus expresses doubt: "And about three o'clock Jesus cried out in a loud voice, *'Eli, Eli, lema sabachthani?'* which means, 'My God, my God, why have you forsaken me?'" (Matthew 27:46-47). Again, Jesus resolves his doubts: "Jesus cried out in a loud voice, 'Father, into your hands I commend my spirit'; and when he had said this he breathed his last" (Luke 23:46).

Even Abraham who had enough faith to obey God and bring his son to the altar as a sacrifice had, at other times in his life, struggled with "unbelief." While he had enough faith to leave Haran and go to Canaan, as God commanded, Abraham struggled with "unbelief" when he felt he had to lie about Sarai to preserve his life in Egypt (Genesis 12:10-20) and when he was prostrate with laughter and disbelief when God told him Sarah would bear him a child when she was ninety and he was a hundred years old (Genesis 17:17).

Living faith, then, is always tested by difficulties, and these difficulties strengthen that faith, as our very lives are strengthened by the many difficulties we face and overcome.

So often we will point to our difficulties or setbacks in life as proof that faith is meaningless, even as proof that God doesn't exist. Equating faith with guarantees of personal gratification, we become disappointed that we don't get what we want or that we face problems. We seem to forget that living faith is not a genie in a bottle, ready at the rubbing to fulfill our wishes. Rather, living faith is a source of strength, fortifying us to cope with our problems, to move forward with courage, and to be useful.

As we become increasingly dependent on advanced technologies, we may also find ourselves believing that we have no need for faith, no need even for God, that we are supermen whose innovations have made faith and God obsolete. At such times, we might consider that this very technology that has given us this false sense of independence from God has also brought us closer to ultimate and final destruction than has any other cataclysmic occurrence in our entire history on earth.

While breakthroughs in technology increase our ability to redesign the world, they have not given us the wisdom to manage this new power. Rather, these new technologies have made us arrogantly and falsely believe that we can "play God," as it were: to take control over space, over the environment, and even over the life and death of unborn children and the elderly. It has made us arrogantly and falsely believe that we can do whatever we want to do, without considering consequences, because we have split the atom, cracked the DNA code, and landed probes on distant planets.

Such a sense of careless power has led to nearly fourteen million infants aborted worldwide, in one year, of which half the number were aborted in China; it has led to widespread overt and covert euthanasia with terminal-care patients; it has led to over ninety million people killed in acts of political genocide in the last century; it has led to nearly 300,000 tons of atomic waste sitting like time bombs in a variety of precarious storage facilities across the globe, and the numbers increase each year; it has led to the food chain being polluted by genetic engineering, and there is no turning back. Some scientists have even proposed that genetically altered food is responsible for a worldwide epidemic in childhood asthma.

Do we really believe, in the face of these crises, that faith and God are obsolete, that we can run this world without faith and without God? Do we really believe that we are in control of our new technologies and that we know what we are doing? Or is the evidence mounting that we need to rely on God more than ever before in our human history? Is the evidence mounting that we cannot point to our difficulties as proof that faith doesn't work but rather that we have to redouble our efforts to build unconditional trust in God and receive the gift of unconditional faith to guide our lives? And is the evidence mounting that we need stories that can inspire and instruct us in the ways of living faith?

Chapter Two

~

The First Born: A Child of Faith

Before I formed you in the womb I knew you.
(Jeremiah 1:5)

It is always in the context of an individual's life and in the context of the times and forces that shape him and his purpose that the life of faith can be most easily revealed. So it is in this particular life of faith, sharply revealed against the realities of the last Great Depression, a catastrophic world war, and religious and social turmoil, and gently revealed in the reflections of a man whose tone and demeanor tell more about faith than anything he may do or say.

This story of faith begins in Upstate New York some eighty years ago, in the hearts of Margaret Campbell and Peter Girzone, the parents of Joseph Francis Girzone; and like so many stories of living faith, it begins with an enormous challenge.

~

Margaret Campbell, the daughter of a devoutly Catholic

French Canadian mother and a Scotch Presbyterian father, was brought up in her mother's faith and became acquainted with God at a very early age. Before she had reached her teens, Margaret had to face a childhood battle with scarlet fever. During this frightening time, her family's prayers and their deep trust in God comforted her and provided her with the support she needed for her recovery. While the disease left her with permanent heart and kidney damage, it left her, also, with the indelible and sustaining experience of God's abundant love and healing grace. This early encounter with God became the cornerstone of Margaret's faith. Throughout her long and productive life, that faith was severely tested, only to grow a little stronger with each test.

In her late teens, Margaret met Peter Girzone, a sincere and caring man whose deep spiritual commitments matched her own. The two fell in love and married and, in short order, Margaret became pregnant with their first child. What joy that pregnancy held for the young couple!

The year was 1929, the year most of us associate with the stock market crash and the beginning of The Great Depression. It was also the year that Adolph Hitler appointed Heinrich Himmler to head the Schutzstaffel, or SS, as the world would soon refer to this elite inner corps of the Nazi Party.

In time, both events would affect their young family but, in September of 1929, the blessings of anticipating their first child far outweighed the dark clouds of economic and political upheaval that surrounded Margaret and Peter Girzone.

The news of Margaret's pregnancy had a very different effect on their family doctor. After Margaret's first visit, the doctor asked that she and Peter meet with him. He was deeply concerned that Margaret's infirmities were so great that neither she nor her infant could survive through pregnancy and childbirth.

How devastating that meeting had been for Margaret and Peter. Under the doctor's stern gaze, they listened intently as he reviewed the damage that Margaret had suffered in her bout with scarlet fever, heart and kidney damage that made her, according to the doctor's diagnosis, too weakened to sustain a normal pregnancy. Next, they heard the prognosis that natural motherhood was something the radiant young bride could simply never hope to enjoy. Then came the final blow, as the doctor presented the startled couple with the only viable medical alternative he could recommend for a woman in her condition: abortion.

Abortion: the word hung in the air like the ominous blade of a guillotine above the head of a condemned man. Abortion: the word pounded like a hammer through Margaret's mind; while Peter, sitting next to her, was stunned, as if by a swift, harsh blow to his head.

Neither Margaret Campbell nor Peter Girzone could ever have anticipated such a moment in their lives. Brought up with traditional Catholic values and constant in their growing faith in God, this young couple could not relate on any level to their doctor's advice. It was not simply that the doctrines of their church strictly forbade abortion. It was that their spiritual temperaments were repelled by the harsh realities of abortion; and their relationship with God and with each other excluded the very concept of abortion. For Margaret and Peter, abortion involved an act of violence against God, an act of willfulness that would destroy their God-given blessing. No matter what the consequences, abortion was simply not an alternative they could seriously consider.

It would be difficult to assess who may have been more

distressed that day: the doctor who was certain his patient and her infant would die if she continued the pregnancy; or Margaret and Peter who had been confronted with a seemingly irrefutable medical recommendation that they were soul-bound to reject.

Were there any special precautions that Margaret could take to ensure her safety or the safety of her child?

The doctor could think of none.

Were there any drugs or remedies that Margaret could use to minimize the dangers she and her child were facing?

The doctor could think of none.

Were there any medical procedures that could be performed to improve the health of either the mother or the child?

The doctor could think of none.

He remained adamant in his recommendation: abortion was the only alternative.

What fears and pain accompanied Margaret and Peter as they left the doctor's office that day? Could anyone really know what they were feeling, even if the couple could find words to express those feelings? Could the couple see, in that dark night, that their faith was being tested, being honed, being shaped and strengthened? Could they anticipate God's purpose for them and for their unborn child at that moment of impact?

Probably not! We rarely can divine God's purpose in the midst of our human struggles. Mary was troubled and frightened at the Annunciation; and Jesus was sweating blood in the garden at Gethsemane; just as we each are troubled and frightened and sweating blood when we are being stretched beyond the boundaries of our human imaginations. Yet God seems to have an uncanny way of never stretching us beyond our true capacity to stretch, only beyond our perception of that capacity. As we are God's own creation, God alone knows our true limitations and abilities. When we open our lives to God, those limitations and abilities are revealed.

For Margaret and Peter, the crisis they faced was not a crisis of faith. They were faith-certain that they would not agree to an abortion. They were faith-certain that their obedience belonged to God, and that God, not the doctor, was their ultimate authority. Their trust in God and their faith were unconditional.

The crisis they faced was a more basic human crisis. They were very young, Margaret just barely twenty; and they were filled with youthful wisdom and dreams. Now, all at once, they were being challenged to be wise beyond their years and courageous beyond their dreams. They were being stretched beyond the boundaries of their own imaginations.

Were they troubled and frightened? They were newlyweds. They longed to have children. Now they had to face a new troubling, frightening dilemma each day. Should Margaret continue to live like a normal young wife, enjoying her new home and the companionship of her new husband? Should she entertain family and friends and socialize with other newlyweds? Should she stay in bed and avoid exertion of any kind, exertion that might further jeopardize her health and the safety of her child? There were no guidelines to follow, and each expert they called upon gave them the same advice: abortion.

Did they sweat blood? Over the nine months of Margaret's pregnancy, fearing the worst while hoping for the best, they had countless Gethsemane moments.

This was, after all, the second time that Margaret was facing a life-threatening condition, and this time her unborn child was at risk as well.

Still, she had been prepared by her childhood brush with death to face this latest challenge. She had been prepared by a wise and merciful God to be filled with faith, to rest in that faith, and in the love of those around her.

With Peter by her side, Margaret prayed. She prayed to the God of her understanding, the God of Abraham, the God who gave her hope that divine intervention might save her child, as Abraham's child had been saved. She prayed to the Son of God, who accepted His Father's will, though he was sweating blood in Gethsemane. And she prayed to a young woman of miraculous courage. She prayed to Mary: Mary, who provided an example of motherhood for her to follow; Mary, who answered "Yes," though she was troubled and frightened.

Through an interminably long nine months, Peter and Margaret prayed faithfully for the Lord's will for themselves and for their child.

~

In that same year, 1929, The Infant Life Preservation Act was passed in England. This amended the existing law and stated that abortion would no longer be considered a felony if it was carried out for the sole purpose of preserving the mother's life. The act stated that it was still illegal to kill a child who was capable of being born alive, and that any child who was twenty-eight weeks old would be considered viable. The decision for performing legal abortion was placed completely in the hands of the doctors, who would determine if the mother's life was threatened by the pregnancy.

~

On May 15, 1930, a baby boy, Joseph Francis, was born to Margaret and Peter Girzone. He was their first child, the first of twelve children to be born to them. He was their faith child; and his birth became, for them, a testament to God's merciful and powerful presence, an affirmation of God's faithfulness in the lives of those who believe in His love and turn their lives to His purpose.

As for the infant, life was as ordinary as an infant's life could be. Unaware that the circumstances of his birth were extraordinary, or that more than the usual amount of celebration and thanksgiving greeted his arrival, he was suckled and slept, gurgled and cried, and, in time, turned over and sat up like every infant has since the beginning of time.

Newborns possess no conscious tools for assessing their environment. Rather like sponges, they absorb whatever surrounds them without evaluation or judgment; and what they absorb, they integrate into their sense of reality. Reacting to that reality, they smile and coo and cry. They reach out and they withdraw.

It is in these earliest months of life that nurture and nature flow together into an emerging personality. If nurture complements nature, that flow is smooth and satisfying to both parents and child. If nurture antagonizes nature, the flow is turbulent and distressing.

For the newborn Joseph, filled with his mother's deep faith from the very conception of his life, these early years of nurturing complemented his calm and trusting nature. If his parents sometimes held him in their arms for extravagantly long periods of time, marveling at God's miracle in their lives, the infant simply absorbed and enjoyed their attention as a natural part of his life. If, at his baptism, his parents were filled with the joy of so great a reward for their ever-deepening faith, the infant absorbed their joy and felt happy and safe in his world. For Margaret and Peter and their infant son, the threads of their faith and the threads of their lives were woven tightly together into a rare family tapestry.

In the years following Joseph's birth, many new threads would be woven into the tapestry, as each of his eleven siblings began to arrive. With the arrival of each child, Margaret and Peter renewed their gratitude for God's gifts and deepened their trust in God's protection. And each child born reminded them of the miracle of their firstborn child, their child of faith, Joseph Francis.

~

For each child born to a family, the experience of that family is different, simply because the very structure of the family, itself, is changed by the arrival of each new child. Parents are changed too, being older and, perhaps, more burdened as subsequent children arrive. The external world into which each child is born is also changing constantly, and the demands of that world make a difference in the lives of both the parents and the children. Then, the circumstances of each child's birth are distinctive, and parents, quite automatically, respond differently to those distinctions.

The firstborn child, particularly, is set apart by his place in the family, traditionally holding a special, unchallenged position of respect and honor. Along with that special position, the firstborn child is often expected to set an example for the siblings that follow and to carry on the family's heritage.

Once the rest of the children begin arriving, most of the parents' attention is, by necessity, diverted to meet the needs of their growing brood. This shift in attention always represents a loss to the firstborn child; and even when carefully explained, this loss of the parents' once absolute and undivided attention always proves baffling and painful for that child. Very often, the first-born experiences this loss as a betrayal by his parents and begins to retreat into the less-confusing world of his own imagination. While in that world, the child may conclude that his loss is the result of something he has done wrong or, worse, the result of something that is intrinsically wrong with him. The younger the firstborn child at the time that the others begin arriving, the more confusing and irrevocable this sense of loss and betrayal will be. Very often that sense of loss and betrayal results in a loss of trust in all figures of authority, both parents and God.

After enjoying such extraordinary amounts of undivided attention and affection from his adoring parents, the sensitive young Joseph, not yet two years old, certainly would have felt a shift in his parents' focus when his siblings began arriving. Although still too young to express his feelings, the young Joseph had a foundation of faith and love so strong that any hurt he may have felt was converted into deeper empathy. Any imagined conclusions he may have come to that he had done something wrong were converted into a desire to please and to try to be more acceptable, more perfect. By nature, trusting and obedient, Joseph continued to grow into a child with a compassionate and caring temperament.

More important, unlike most children whose trust in God can often be confused with trust in their parents, Joseph did not suffer any such confusion; for Joseph had established a very separate and personal relationship with God before he was born. In her prayers and in her quiet times, Margaret had created a bond between her unborn infant and a loving God. Margaret and Peter continued building that bond after their son was born. They spoke of Jesus, as one speaks of an especially caring and cherished member of the family. They prayed together to a loving Jesus, and they prayed with unquestioning trust that their prayers were being received. The relationship they fostered between their son and Jesus was a living, vital friendship, a friendship he could always rely on.

Margaret and Peter also shared with Joseph their deep devotion to Mary. Through their acts of reverence, they taught him of Mary's obedience and faithfulness and, especially, of her unconditional *fiat*, her willingness to trust God and her conscious consent to receive God's will for her. And they taught him that he could always rely on the Holy Mother's protection.

From the day of Joseph's baptism, Margaret and Peter were equally painstaking in introducing their son to the Church, its laws, its rituals, and its sacred function in the life of every Christian. And they set an example for him by their own conscientious involvement with their local parish.

As year by year the Girzone family grew, Joseph listened and watched as his parents repeated their messages of faith for each of his siblings; and every time Joseph heard those messages repeated, it reinforced his own faith and strengthened his deepening attraction to Jesus and His Church.

Throughout his childhood, and especially in the lonely times – and there were so many lonely times in his home, filled with all his exuberant siblings, each heading full tilt in a different direction – young Joseph always enjoyed the gentle companionship with Jesus that his parents had established for him. He was able to find comfort in his innate and growing faith in God's love; and it was to Jesus and His Mother that Joseph always turned with his deepest hurts and fears, his most cherished hopes and dreams.

On an intuitive level, not yet fully defined in his young mind, Joseph was coming to understand the distinction between the limited reach of human love and the infinite reaches of God's love.

~

Joseph was two years old when he first became attracted to the priesthood. He was at that age when children imperiously imagine themselves omnipotent, demanding total independence and total attention at the same time. With their new interest in clothes, in dressing up and acting like their parents, and in being treated as an authoritative member of the family, these charming two year olds are often mistaken for being mature beyond their years. Still not fully developed physically and walking a bit hunched over, they look in so many ways like wise old men.

One minute, these miniature adults will fancy themselves heroic astronauts; the next minute, they will be football heroes or brave firemen. All the while, they are exploring the world and trying to define their place in life. For some, these early explorations develop, in time, into mature choices. For most, they last only through childhood.

Peter Girzone must have enjoyed his two-year-old's innocent determination to be grown up. After Mass one Sunday morning, Joseph pointed to the man in the long black robe:

"Who's that?" he tugged gently at his father.

"That's the priest," Peter patiently explained.

"That's what I'm going to be," declared the young

Joseph, in a definitive and resolute tone of voice.

Certainly, Margaret and Peter would have been delighted with their son's attraction to the priesthood. Perhaps Margaret, in her private talks with God during her pregnancy, may have promised this child to God's service. That would not be unusual. Perhaps his family's respect and admiration for the priest influenced the young Joseph. Perhaps it was simply the fanciful imaginings of a two-year-old. Or, perhaps, God had chosen Joseph Francis before he was born.

Chapter Three

~

Attractions and Distractions: The Formative Years

I formed you to be a servant to me....
(Isaiah 44:21)

A world full of contradictions surrounded young Joseph as he grew. In the same year that this tender two-year-old child was becoming fascinated with his parish priest, that man in the long black robe, another man, a man with a bristly moustache and slicked-down black hair, was gaining control of the Reichstag, the legislative assembly of pre-Nazi Germany. The Japanese had invaded China, killing a Buddhist priest in Shanghai and occupying Manchuria; and the United States had just charged Japan with the violation of the Open Door Policy.

Around the dinner table in the Girzone household, Joseph heard little of these events. Americans were much more concerned, at that time, with the Great Depression which was raging through the nation, and through Europe, like an uncontrollable plague. In America, alone, unemployment figures had reached an average of twelve million jobless a month, and Franklin Delano Roosevelt had just been elected president on the Democratic ticket, promising to make things better with his New Deal programs.

~

Peter Girzone was more fortunate than many. He owned a successful butcher shop near Albany, the state capitol of New York, and he had a loyal clientele who knew they would always get the best meat available when they came to his shop. Peter was sincere, conscientious, and unassuming, and his customers enjoyed doing business with him.

Nevertheless, Peter had to work very hard and live very modestly in order to meet the needs of his growing family. In his formative years, the young Joseph often had a taste of the stark severity of a worldwide economic collapse. The Great Depression was a daily reminder of just how unreliable all material security could be; and Peter Girzone taught Joseph that lesson by example, by the way he lived, and by the way he placed his own faith in God's protection and love.

Joseph absorbed those early lessons from his father, and much later on, in his adult life, at a time when all he possessed in the world was his faith, he would have the opportunity to put those lessons to the test.

~

The popular view that childhood is an idyllic state, free of pain and confusion, is, in fact, a sentimental distortion of one of the most painful and confusing stages of our lives. We are, as children, "too little and too small" to alter our circumstances, and no matter how important and real our feelings and insights are to us, we are often told, directly or indirectly, that those feelings and insights are not of much consequence. To make matters worse, we have only fragments of information about ourselves and our world with which to try to make sense of what we are really feeling and what is really happening to us.

In adulthood, on the other hand, no matter how weak and confused we may feel, we have the ability to gather all the information we need to understand our problems. We can make and execute choices, and we can find ways to handle the consequences of those choices. More important, we have the perspective of experiences which we can use to assess our feelings about ourselves and others.

The more perceptive we are as children, the more uncomfortable and self-conscious we become, as we try to understand who we are in relation to our peers and as we try to align what we feel with what we are being told.

Keenly perceptive and shy as a child, Joseph faced these struggles bravely. He found little comfort with his playmates; and as one neighborhood friend moved away or another ignored him or treated him carelessly, he accepted over and over again the acute pain of loss and separation. He found most of his peers to be frivolous and careless, lacking his sensitivities and compassion. To protect himself, he made a silent, instinctive decision to keep his deepest feelings to himself, and he began to spend much of his free time in the company of his own imagination, abounding with his private dreams and secrets.

The years between two and four are often called the "little adolescence." For young Joseph, those years were much more than a dress rehearsal for the real thing. Emotionally responsive beyond his age level, he experienced the isolation, the alienation, the identity crisis, and many of the social conflicts that characterize the teen years. These experiences profoundly affected him, creating a disquieting dialogue between his soul and his personality that, in years to come, would help define the course of his life.

As an adult, Joseph reflected on this period of his childhood in his book, *Never Alone*:

> I learned very young that I was alone in a world where everyone seemed a stranger, and that you could not hold on to even those you loved. They only too easily slipped away from you. And even more painful, there was no assurance that those I loved loved me in return. People impressed me as being without feeling. They just laughed and talked, and said funny things that made others laugh, but had no real feeling for one another.[3]

His poignant words echo the sentiments of Somerset Maugham in his autobiographical novel, *Of Human Bondage*:

> The new-born child does not realise that his body is more a part of himself than surrounding objects, and will play with his toes without any feeling that they belong to him more than the rattle by his side; and it is only by degrees, through pain, that he understands the fact of the body. And experiences of the same kind are necessary for the individual to become conscious of himself; but here there is a difference that, although everyone becomes equally conscious of himself as a separate and complete organism, everyone does not become equally conscious of himself as a complete and

separate personality.[4]

Maugham, through his hero, Philip Carey, goes on to describe the "social animal":

The feeling of apartness from others comes to most with puberty, but it is not always developed to such a degree as to make the difference between the individual and his fellows noticeable to the individual. It is such as he, as little conscious of himself as the bee in a hive, who are the lucky in life, for they have the best chance of happiness: their activities are shared by all, and their pleasures are only pleasures because they are enjoyed in common; you will see them on Whit-Monday dancing on Hampstead Hall, shouting at a football match, or from club windows in Pall Mall cheering a royal procession. It is because of them that man has been called a social animal.[5]

For Philip Carey, the passage "from the innocence of childhood to bitter consciousness of himself"[6] was the result of ridicule he suffered because of his club foot. For young Joseph, there was no such marked physical deformity, no apparent difference between himself and his peers. Why then, before he was even five years old, had he already experienced "bitter consciousness of himself"?

What set Joseph apart from his peers was a very different kind of cross. Set apart, automatically, by the circumstances of his birth, Joseph was also set apart by his rare God-given spiritual gifts: his innate faith and his gentle compassion. Slowly, he would come to understand these gifts as he grew to maturity; but for so young a child, these gifts proved a heavy burden.

~

During those unsettling years of his early childhood, Joseph found that his truly best friend was God. God was constant, always at his side. God heard his deepest thoughts, his dreams, and his secrets. God never disappointed him or betrayed him or abandoned him. God seemed to care about him, appreciate him, and understand everything he was feeling. So young Joseph hung out with God.

His First Communion was a time of great joy for Joseph. Now he would have the chance to get even closer to Jesus. He took seriously his first time in the confessional, searching out and enumerating his youthful sins, mortal and venial. He had become very demanding of himself and was often the harshest judge of his transgressions; and he performed his acts of penance with heartfelt remorse.

He would spend as much time as he could with Jesus. Walking alone to church each morning for daily Mass, kneeling at the altar rail to receive Holy Communion, and lingering on in the quiet church after the Mass was over, he felt the presence of Jesus. And in ways he could not define, that presence gave him courage. With God at his side, he could accept, rather than deny, the pain and isolation he was feeling, and he could continue to respond to the joy and to the pain in the world around him.

As Joseph stayed close to God, so God stayed close to Joseph. The benevolent God who had given Joseph his special gifts would make certain that this lovable young child would never walk alone with those gifts.

~

One of the Four Noble Truths in Buddhism states that life is suffering. In the spiritual wisdom of most religions, such suffering results from our natural struggle with our separation from God. In our understanding of human development, we also observe this suffering being generated by resisitance to primal, maternal separations at birth and in childhood. When, in the course of our lives, we confront these natural, human struggles, we begin to grow toward personal fulfillment. When, on the other hand, we try to escape our struggles and put our efforts toward avoiding suffering, we find ourselves unsatisfied, anxious, and neurotic. Running from intimacy with ourselves, we become incapable of intimacy with others, seeking only external, momentary gratifications.

We are always being challenged, then, to embrace our struggles, to reach out for God in our suffering, to be transformed by God's healing love, and to fulfill God's creative purpose in our lives.

While Joseph had sensed, very early in his life, that he was different from his peers, he was much too young to be able to analyze why he was so different. And he had no way of understanding why his peers did not seem to feel the pain that he often felt. On the contrary, like most people, they seemed to avoid any thought or activity that might prove painful. If they did experience anything painful, they seemed to bury it or to act silly or nasty to cover what they were feeling.

As much as his innate faith had so fundamentally set him apart from others, it was Joseph's willingness, at so young an age, to accept pain and to suffer life's problems that, more than anything, made this separation so acute.

He was set apart, also, by his attraction to God. His peers did not seek out time with God as he did. Rather, they seemed to always be running around, never sitting still long enough to be with God. They seemed to avoid God, just as they avoided pain.

Although he was set apart by his unique spiritual gifts, as well, Joseph had no conscious awareness of those gifts. Nor did he have any awareness of his obedient and responsive nature. With no accurate reflection of his soul or his personality available to him, he soon came to the conclusion that he was strange, that he was the one out of step in life's parade.

It takes a very long time for us to come to know ourselves and to see that we have within us beautiful souls that God has created. As children, we are usually too distracted by measuring ourselves against our peers, or judging ourselves by the reflections we garner from the adults in our world. And although parents, naturally, love their children, very few are detached enough from their own concerns to see and encourage the true nature of a child. Even when, as children, we are in the presence of God, sensing that God knows and loves us as we are, we usually cannot see ourselves as God sees us, nor can we love ourselves as God loves us.

Although young Joseph spent countless hours with God and felt strengthened and uplifted by God's presence, he had not yet developed the tools he needed to realize the beauty of his own soul. He was deeply attracted to his comforting friendship with God; but he was also continually distracted by his self doubts and a nagging belief that he was not worthy of God's unconditional love. He was emotionally and spiritually courageous, but he had no sense of his courage or how that courage would help shape the person he was to become. And he had no way of knowing how pleasing he was to God.

Nevertheless, throughout his childhood, as throughout his life, Joseph's unyielding faith in God's love and wisdom would provide comfort when little else did. In time, Joseph would come to understand his gifts and come to know the nature of his soul; but that would be much later in his life, after many trials and many years of relentless emotional pain.

~

Young Joseph's attraction to religious life grew deeper as he grew older. He spent as much time as possible in his parish church. It became his home away from home, a private haven away from the noisy, incessant comings and goings of his siblings, the family friends, and relatives.

Joseph loved everything about the church: the sweet aroma of incense mingling with burnished wood; the hushed, solemn silence; the sun-drenched stained glass windows, alive with biblical heroes; the awe-inspiring statues of Mary and Joseph; even the cold, hard wooden pews. Most of all, he loved the church because he could be near Jesus: on the Crucifix; in the Stations of the Cross; and, especially, in the Blessed Sacrament.

A two-year-old Joseph had been drawn to the repetitive rituals and routines of the church, the cadence of the Latin Mass, and the recurring phrases of hymns and prayers. As he grew older, he was sustained by the reliable rhythms of the holy year. He looked forward to all the holy days that marked the life, the death, and the resurrection of his beloved Jesus; and he, particularly, enjoyed sharing those special times of worship and celebration with his family.

An avid reader, young Joseph soon discovered the lives of the saints. He savored every detail as he read and reread their stories. The virtues of the early Christian martyrs, especially, captured his imagination. Their ascetic devotion, their emotional endurance, their prolonged suffering, their imitation of Christ in death: these unconditional sacrifices opened a whole new world of possibilities to him. With his singular attraction to Jesus and his youthful and intense idealism, Joseph could identify with those men and women who had so passionately and totally given their lives to love and to serve the Lord. He admired their radical grace and their good works. Most of all he admired their spiritual perfection. They were his heroes.

By the time Joseph was ten years old, he had determined, in his own mind, that he would someday be a saint, like one of his heroes; and he set his sights on becoming a priest. The attraction of the two-year-old child had developed into the dream of a young boy; and Joseph announced his intentions to his family.

Chapter Four

~

Hair Shirts and Humility

I have been most zealous for the Lord,
the God of hosts....
(1 Kings 19:10)

The year was 1940. The German army, which had been marching unchecked across Europe, had reached Paris and set up the Vichy government in France, while the free French forces under Charles de Gaulle were fighting the Germans in West Africa. The Nazi Luftwaffe was bombing London, and Italian forces were attacking the British in North Africa. The Japanese were continuing their aggression in China, occupying French Indochina, and the Soviets had forced the surrender of Finland. In America, Roosevelt was re-elected; and in Britain, Winston Churchill became the new prime minister.

The year before, in 1939, Britain and France had declared war on Germany, after the Nazis invaded Poland. America had not yet joined forces with the Allies, but our involvement seemed imminent. By 1941, the Selective Service System started to gear up for our entry into the war, repealing a bill limiting the army to

900,000 men and extending the length of service to a minimum of eighteen months. That same year, Roosevelt and Churchill met secretly to frame the Atlantic Charter, vowing to destroy the Nazi threat; and America sent troops to Iceland to defend against a possible attack. In the desert at Los Alamos, New Mexico, the highly classified Manhattan Project was launched, and teams of internationally renowned scientists were brought together to begin their top-secret research to build an atomic bomb.

Before the end of 1941, the German submarines would sink two U.S. destroyers, the *Kearny* and the *Reuben James*, and more than a hundred American lives would be lost. Two thousand more American lives would be lost on December 7, when the Japanese naval and air forces launched a surprise attack on the U.S. naval base at Pearl Harbor in Hawaii, forcing America to declare war on Japan. Germany and Italy would respond by declaring war on America; and Congress would pass a resolution recognizing a state of war against these nations. By Christmas Day, 1941, America was at war on all fronts.

The following year, the draft age was lowered to eighteen and food and raw materials needed for the war effort were being strictly rationed. The nation had been mobilized, and in one way or another, the war reached into every American home.

~

Joseph was not yet twelve years old, the eldest of the family's nine children, at the time his father was drafted. In *Never Alone*, he recalls that time vividly:

> Reporters came to the house for interviews. They asked my father if he was angry for being drafted, since

he had an army of his own to care for. "No," he said. "There are times when we must fulfill our duty to our country." "But who will take care of your wife and all your children?" one of the reporters asked. To which my father replied, "If God can use me to take care of them, He can do just as good a job without me."[7]

What a profound, yet frightening, day that was for young Joseph. On the one hand, Peter Girzone had shown admirable strength, setting a standard for unquestioning faith and courage for his son to follow. On the other hand, Joseph was being confronted with the possibility of losing his father; and, if his father were sent overseas, there would be no guarantee that he would safely return. A crisis half way across the globe was threatening to dispassionately cut Joseph off from the supportive relationship that every twelve-year-old boy hopes to build with his father. If his father went to war, the hope of building that relationship could never be fully recovered.

Certainly, Joseph and his family would survive if Peter left for war; and God would continue to companion young Joseph, in any event. But there were things that an emerging adolescent could not really ask God, new stirrings about the measure of a man and the nature of manhood. A young boy relies on his father to lend him a hand as he explores these new frontiers; and in a million and one subtle and unspoken ways, a son looks to his father to help him gauge his progress through this transition. For Joseph, a world war could, swiftly and carelessly, deprive him of that support. Although he was keenly aware of the threat of losing his father, the twelve-year-old Joseph had no way of knowing all the new, undefined ways in which he would need his father's encouragement during so crucial a phase in his development. Courageous as ever, Joseph determined, on the day that his father was drafted, that he would suffer whatever loss came his way.

Mercifully, Joseph was spared that loss. When Peter showed up for his physical, the draft board discovered that he suffered with varicose veins, and they concluded that this condition disqualified him for the army. The Girzone family accepted the good news in stride and went back to their normal routines; and responding from the perspective of his own reality, Peter tried, to the best of his ability, to support his eldest son's dreams and understand the yearnings of his unique personality. For young Joseph, however, the entire incident was one more convincing reminder of the lesson he had learned so early in his life: "that you could not hold on to those you loved." So, standing on the bedrock of his living faith, Joseph continued to concentrate on his journey toward God.

~

While Joseph was putting all his efforts toward making himself worthy of God's love, God was walking by his side, teaching him, in many small ways, the lessons He wanted Joseph to learn.

It was Good Friday in 1942, the year that Peter Girzone was drafted. Joseph, devotedly, was trying to observe three hours of silence in honor of Christ's passion. He became restless before the time was up and began to wander off down the road. As he had grown to be very demanding of himself, he felt badly that he was unable to sit still for the full three hours.

Disappointed and downcast, he aimlessly came upon an

abandoned building and went inside to explore the basement. There he discovered several huge piles of old, forgotten books. As if led by God's own hand, he reached in and pulled out one particular book that caught his eye. He took it out into the light, and thumbing through its stained and faded pages, he found a story that so profoundly affected him that, to this day, he relates its message:

There was once a wealthy French family who lived in a chateau on the outskirts of Paris. They kept all their money hidden in the basement. One day, the family's butler found the hiding place, and within days, the butler murdered the entire family, one by one, except for the youngest son who overheard the screams of his parents and siblings and ran into the woods to safety.

Now an orphan, the young boy entered a seminary and, years later, he became a priest, assigned as the chaplain at Devil's Island. The butler had continued his life of crime, was eventually caught, and was now serving his life sentence, also at Devil's Island. One day, the chaplain was called into the field to minister to a dying inmate. It was the butler. "Don't waste your time, Father," the butler begged. "I have done so many bad things that God can never forgive me." The chaplain encouraged the dying man to tell his story. When the butler had finished, the priest said: "I am the young boy whose family you murdered. If I can forgive you, certainly God can forgive you; and I forgive you with my whole heart."[8]

That story spoke to the young Joseph, as if it had been written just for him to discover that very day. It spoke to him of the depth of compassion and forgiveness that a merciful God shows to all His children, a compassion similar to the compassion Joseph had always felt for others – and a compassion and forgiveness that God, Himself, on that Good Friday afternoon, was showing to a lonely and downcast Joseph, who was judging himself and his sacrifice as unworthy.

~

During that same eventful year of 1942, a Carmelite friar, Titus Brandsma, was martyred in the Nazi concentration camp at Dachau for his anti-Nazi sentiments and for his work with the Catholic journalists of the Netherlands. An institute of spirituality would be named in his honor at the University of Nijmegen where he had taught. And, in 1985, he would be named Blessed by Pope John Paul II.

At Auschwitz, that same year, St. Teresa Benedicta of the Cross, a Carmelite nun, was also martyred. Her given name was Edith Stein. A native of Germany and a Jewish convert to Catholicism, St. Teresa Benedicta was a brilliant philosopher, teacher, lecturer, and writer. Twelve years old and unaware of her martyrdom at the time it occurred, Joseph, decades later when he became a priest, would be a founding member of the Edith Stein Guild and a sponsor for her beatification in 1987.

~

At the age of fourteen, Joseph entered St. Albert's, a Carmelite seminary nestled in the rolling foothills of the Catskill Mountains in Middletown, New York. It was 1944. Several years before, he had met a Carmelite priest at his aunt's house. The priest captured his interest, and whenever they would meet again, they would speak about Joseph's vocation.

To the Carmelite, young Joseph must have seemed a rare soul. At an early age, he appeared to have developed a contemplative temperament: he cherished solitude and silence; he had developed a deep inner life; he was eager to be pleasing to God; and he was intensely attracted to Jesus. All these qualities would make him particularly well suited to Carmelite spirituality. Beyond these attributes, his most striking quality was his profound, unwavering faith, his willingness to trust God, and, under all circumstances, to answer "Yes" to God's plan for him.

~

Founded at Mount Carmel in 1200 AD, the Carmelites attributed their spiritual roots to the prophet Elijah, who confronted the Israelites at Mount Carmel, and to Mary, whose chapel was said to be situated at Mount Carmel, where the first hermitages originated. Here the the prescribed Rule for the monks required living in silence and in solitude in individual cells, the continual praying of the psalms, and a life centered on following Jesus. Before the end of the thirteenth century, in keeping with the trend set by the Franciscan and Dominican orders, this Rule had expanded to include both living in solitude within Carmelite communities and a commitment to pastoral ministry.

In modern times, Carmelite spirituality strongly reflected the reforms introduced by St. Teresa of Avila and St. John of the Cross. Working under the critical eye of the Inquisition in sixteenth-century Spain, St. Teresa and St. John revised the Order and advanced the mystical experience springing from its contemplative tradition. Their writings further established a union with God in love as the primary goal of modern Carmelite spirituality. In that union, God's loving actions work in our lives to transform us, liberate us from attachments that keep us bound, and free us to love God and love one another as we are loved by God.

~

Filled with the innocent passion and the unyielding idealism of a young seminarian of fourteen, Joseph Francis fervently committed himself to following the Carmelite path toward an unconditional and absolute union with God in love.

~

The war that was shattering the world was just beginning to show signs of ending the year Joseph entered St. Albert's. Blackouts were being relaxed in Britain; and in America, rationing of all but the choicest cuts of beef had ended. The Allied invasion of Normandy on D-Day, June 6, 1944, had driven back the German defense lines; U.S. planes had infiltrated German lines and were bombing Berlin; and U.S. ground troops had driven the Germans out of Rome.

Roosevelt had been re-elected for a fourth term, with Harry Truman as his vice president. At the Dumbarton Oaks Conference, delegates from America, the U.S.S.R., and the British Commonwealth were proposing the creation of a permanent international peace-keeping organization to be called the United Nations.

The Allied efforts in the Pacific were being led by Generals MacArthur and Stilwell.

At Los Alamos, New Mexico, the scientists were less than a year away from exploding the first atomic test bomb in the desert, near Alamogordo. J. Robert Oppenheimer, heading the Weapons Laboratory for the Manhattan Project, believed that the destructive power of the bomb would be a deterrent to aggression, and that the bomb would, ultimately, become an instrument of world peace. He and his team named the bomb "Trinity."

~

Engaged in a very different kind of war, a young seminarian was searching for a very different kind of peace in a private struggle of his own, a struggle for his soul.

The call to the priesthood was a personal one for each of the young seminarians at St. Albert's. For some, the attraction was to pastoral ministry; for others, to monastic life; and for still others, to missionary work. For some, like Joseph Francis, the attraction was love.

Joseph entered St. Albert's intent on sacrificing his total being to the love of God. He longed to perfect himself spiritually, to become holy, and to come closer to God through a strict and unyielding observance of God's commandments.

Joseph prayed earnestly that God would help him achieve this perfection. And he prayed, especially, to develop that ultimate discipline and obedience that marked the lives of the saints. Only with such saintly perfection did he feel he could be fully acceptable to God.

~

Perhaps no single subject engages the attention and the energies of the human mind and heart more than the subject of love. From Deuteronomy to Corinthians, from Electra to Freud, from the Kamasutra to Masters and Johnson, the whole of recorded history is entwined with our longing to comprehend love's mysteries.

Historically, the definitions of love are as varied as the cultures and people who sought to define it: the ideal love of Plato; the sensual love of Ovid; the spiritual love of Christianity; the courtly love of the troubadours; and, then, romantic love, embellished with rapture and adventure, spanning all ages and all civilizations.

Common to all these definitions of love is the disturbing conflict that we often experience between the real and the ideal, between body and soul, between aloneness and oneness. The deep desire of the human heart to overcome this conflict has translated, down through the ages, as a desire to achieve unity with the beloved and to create, through that unity, a mystical "oneness of being," a psychological and spiritual "center."

As each society developed, that society added its prescription for achieving this perfect union in love, until, looking back through the centuries, we find that we have a vast pharmacopoeia of prescriptions to choose from.

Nevertheless, after more than six thousand years of recorded existence, the human heart still struggles with love. Modern statistics tell us that over ninety-eight percent of all our relationships are dysfunctional, while a vast majority of our population complains of unprecedented alienation and loneliness.

Have we simply failed to find, in the prescriptions of the past, a definition of love that meets our needs? Do we need a new prescription? Or does this very struggle to find a perfect union in love define our humanity?

~

From the moment he entered St. Albert's, young Joseph drove himself relentlessly toward his goal. Throughout his childhood, he had enjoyed a deep, trusting relationship with Jesus. Jesus was his protector, his confidant, and his friend. Now he longed for that relationship to grow even deeper. As a seminarian, he determined that he would seek every opportunity available to bring himself closer to God.

Loving God in the only way he knew how to love, the way he had been taught as a child, Joseph pursued his dream. He began each day at dawn, going outdoors to immerse himself in God's glorious creation. He thanked God for the beauty that surrounded him, from the vast expanse of pastel sky to the tiniest drop of sparkling dew slowly evaporating into the morning mist.

He became meticulous in his prayer life and strict in his participation in the liturgy. Through all his waking hours, he labored to shut himself off from any distraction, disciplining his mind and heart to concentrate only on the Lord. He spent days contemplating the life of Jesus, His Death, and His Resurrection. Whenever his rigorous program at the seminary permitted, he knelt before the Blessed Sacrament for hours in adoration and thanksgiving.

Immersed in the doctrine of original sin, he judged himself a sinner, unworthy of God's love. He diligently and daily enumerated his mortal and venial sins. Inexhaustible in the scrutiny of his thoughts and his behavior, he suffered with the ambiguities of his human desires and his spiritual goals. And the more he suffered, the more he persevered in his penance.

Methodically, he left no stone unturned in his quest for a more intimate relationship with God.

Joseph was now fifteen, and at the end of his first year at St. Albert's. A few of his fellow seminarians had decided not to return the following year. They considered themselves unsuitable for clerical life, either not sufficiently devout or, simply, emotionally unfit for the calling.

Joseph wondered whether he, too, was unfit for the calling. After a year of rigorous academic study, he found himself an able student, but his even more rigorous pursuit of his spiritual goals had left him painfully disappointed with his progress. And his disappointment fed into a growing sense of despair.

He had entered the seminary with deep commitments and impassioned dreams. He had applied himself, body and soul, to fulfilling those commitments and to realizing those dreams. He had done everything he knew how to do and everything he was being taught to do. Whatever duties his superiors asked him to perform, he performed willingly and with enthusiasm. And he volunteered whenever he could to do even more. Yet the harder he tried, the further he seemed to slip away from his goals.

He longed to be pleasing to God, to root out his sins and perfect his self-discipline; but after a year of prayer and penitence, he felt himself no less sinful, no less distracted. He longed to pursue holiness with all the energy and exuberance of his young heart, but holiness eluded him. And he longed to come closer to God; but, for the first time in his young life, his constant companion seemed to have abandoned him.

Loneliness had never been a stranger to Joseph. In that loneliness, Joseph had come to rely on the compassionate and steadfast presence of Jesus. Now when he was lonely, he could not sense that presence. And loneliness, without Jesus, was nearly unbearable.

Confused and aching, he reached out for help. He petitioned his spiritual director. His director nodded but gave him no relief. He read and reread the lives of the saints and his spiritual life books looking for clues. He found none! Hoping Jesus would speak to him through the sermons and through the readings at Mass, he tried to listen even more intently for the voice of his beloved. He heard nothing! Afraid they would find him odd, he could not risk discussing his feelings with his peers; so he walked among them, forlorn and dejected, longing always for a sign that he was not alone. There were no such signs! In his loneliness, he cried out for Jesus. There was no answer!

~

American soldiers were beginning to return home. The rationing of shoes, butter, and tires had been lifted in the United States; and, in Europe, the war was nearing its end. It was 1945.

President Roosevelt had suffered a fatal cerebral hemorrhage on April 12, while vacationing at his retreat in Warm Springs, Georgia. Less than a month later, reports out of Germany indicated that Hitler had committed suicide in the Reich's Chancellery; and on May 7, in Rheims, France, the Germans signed a document of unconditional surrender.

In the Pacific, the Japanese continued to fight, rejecting the terms of unconditional surrender.

Americans, electrified by the Allied victory in Europe and the safe return of many of their loved ones, began to celebrate. Parades filled the main streets in every town from Maine to California, and neighbors joined neighbors in parties that lasted for days.

By early August, President Harry Truman ordered an atomic bomb to be dropped on Hiroshima. When Japan continued to resist surrender, a plutonium bomb was dropped on Nagasaki. On August 14, Japan finally agreed to the terms of unconditional surrender.

World War II had officially ended.

Statistics of war casualties on both sides, including military personnel and civilians, were estimated at over fifty-five million dead. At least two million more were reported wounded.

A year later, the Atomic Energy Commission would be established, and five years later, in 1950, President Truman would authorize the building of a hydrogen bomb.

~

Joseph Francis, after much soul-searching, decided to continue on at St. Albert's. His decision, while firm, did little to alleviate his doubts or his growing sense of disappointment with himself. Nevertheless, he was determined to do battle for at least another year. Perhaps he had been too lax or too slow in applying himself and would need to reach deeper and exert greater effort to realize his goals. He prayed that was the case. And he prayed to regain his familiar companionship with Jesus.

Joseph spent many long, hard hours considering his dilemma. Perhaps, if he redoubled his efforts at prayer – perhaps, if he embraced greater suffering – perhaps, if he could learn more about the wisdom of the saints – perhaps, then, he could perfect himself spiritually and be worthy of God's graces. He pledged himself to these goals.

He added hours of prayers to his days; he scrutinized his actions and his thoughts; and he engaged in rigorous acts of penance. He avoided all physical comfort and devised ways to imitate the suffering the saints had endured. Collecting the hair from the floor of the seminary barber shop, he fashioned a hair shirt and wore it day and night, never scratching to relieve his discomfort. He slept on wooden boards placed on top of his mattress. He ate only foods he disliked for months on end. He took cold showers even in the dead of winter, and he sat on straight-backed hard chairs while he studied for hours each night.

If he were to grow closer to God, he would have to persevere in this austere mortification until every thought and action was purified, until every natural impulse was under control. He would have to persevere until every distraction was erased and he hungered only for God's love.

To help him further in his quest, he would delve deeper into the works of the saints, especially the two Carmelite Doctors of the Church, St. John of the Cross and St. Teresa of Avila. He was, by now, totally familiar with the stories of their lives. Second only to the Gospels, those stories were his greatest inspiration; but he felt he needed more. He thirsted for greater insight into the path to spiritual perfection. He knew he could find that insight in their writings. He was, in particular, drawn to St. John's *Dark Night of the Soul* and St. Teresa's *Interior Castle*. He knew from his readings that these two great saints had been friends and had worked together to illuminate the nature of the soul. Each saint, reflecting a distinctly different and individual spiritual nature, had charted the path of the soul on its journey toward perfect union with God. Joseph was certain that their revelations would help illuminate his own darkness and give him the answers he was searching for.

Again, he sought his director's guidance. Again, he was

discouraged. He was told that the works of these great saints were too deep for his discernment, too mystical for his youthful disposition to handle, that he would become confused and distressed, "go over the edge," if he were exposed to the mysteries these writings revealed. He was told to wait until he was older, not as impressionable, and a seasoned student of theology. His discussion with his director left him disappointed and bewildered, in a turmoil of unsettling emotions. He felt anxious, alienated, isolated, misunderstood. And he was angry.

Worst of all, he felt a deep sense of shame. Why were his needs so different, so bitterly unacceptable? Why could he find no way to meet those needs? Surely, he concluded, he was wrong to have such needs. Surely, there must be something intrinsically wrong with him. Surely, once again, he was out of step in life's parade!

His feelings were excruciatingly painful, but they were not new. They had plagued him since childhood.

But, this time, Jesus was not there to comfort him. For nearly fourteen years, Jesus had been his protector, his sanctuary. Jesus understood and accepted his needs and always helped him meet those needs. Now Jesus was gone and, try as he would, Joseph could not find his way back to his beloved companion.

Joseph determined, nevertheless, to go on. His director had not prohibited him from continuing his search; he had merely discouraged him. The treasured works were available in the library, and Joseph managed to find the time in his demanding schedule to begin his explorations.

Drawn to the forthright wit and contemplative spirituality of St. Teresa, Joseph poured over her writings. Her words gave his aching heart some relief and enlightened his soul; and her utterly irrepressible adoration of Jesus renewed his hope. Though he was distracted by his loneliness and youthful impulses, St. Teresa offered hope that those distractions would, in time, fade. Though he felt isolated and unable to feel God's presence, she offered hope that he would be reunited, in time, with that presence. Though he was feeling shame and frustration because of the pace of his spiritual growth, St. Teresa's words assured him that God was infinitely patient and infinitely loving. Her prayers and mystical writings shed light on his own nature, his struggles, and his path. Although far from where he hoped to travel, he was encouraged to continue his journey.

Joseph, likewise, found valuable insights in reading St. John of the Cross. In *Dark Night of the Soul,* particularly, he recognized the anguish of his own soul and his great hunger to be purged of his weaknesses and his sins and to become more pleasing to God. However, the feisty, lyrical, tambourine-playing St. Teresa appealed much more to the struggling fifteen-year-old seminarian than the melancholy, intellectually abstruse St. John; and Joseph continued to absorb her spiritual gifts.

~

If life, with all its trials, is the crucible in which God's love transforms our souls, then youth, surely, is the crucible in which we are primed for that transformation. The impatience of youth, by itself, can catapult us toward trials that can melt down the most headstrong and the most stubborn among us. Fueled by high-octane idealism and ironclad dreams, we will often speed, impatiently, toward those dreams, expecting, it would seem, to blast through concrete walls and go on to reach our destination on the first try. A loving God is the only protection we have to keep us from hurting ourselves when, to our surprise, we hit those unyielding walls. With our youthful sense of omnipotence, we will continue careening toward our dreams, time and time again, until, one day, sufficiently discouraged, and sufficiently bruised from hitting the wall, we walk away, utterly defeated, wondering what we are doing wrong, why we are still so far from our destination.

That's the day that God has been patiently waiting for. It is the day when we begin to experience meltdown in the crucible of our youth.

In time, by trial and error, we learn to accept the pace at which we grow and realize our dreams. And we learn to appreciate the painstaking process by which we transform. With our youthful impatience behind us, we can begin to develop true patience, the kind of patience we need to courageously endure uncertainty and discomfort while God guides us, in His time, toward His purpose.

~

At the end of his second year at St. Albert's, Joseph was still plagued by unrelenting doubts, persistent loneliness, and a growing sense of despair. Still his determination to continue on his path was stronger than ever. He desired no other life for himself. With escalating expectations of achieving perfection and mounting disappointments with his chronic humanity, Joseph was careening along on a crash course, and he was headed for a serious and debilitating collision.

Surprisingly, in the midst of all this turmoil, Joseph was also beginning to respect himself, if not for his holiness or for his spiritual progress, then, at least, for his tenacity and for his very hard-earned self-discipline. Not nearly the great spiritual leap he had hoped to make, nevertheless, these small gifts gave him some sense of satisfaction and self-worth.

And although Joseph began to suspect that the tenderness of his childhood companionship with Jesus might never return, he unconditionally believed that God, in His infinite wisdom and love, knew precisely what He was doing. With living faith, Joseph held on courageously to that belief.

Chapter Five

~

The Sword of Jesus

You shall not have other gods besides me.
(Deuteronomy 5:7)

As God is love, so faith is the gate through which love enters. And our willingness to trust is the key to opening that gate. When we are willing to receive God's gift of faith and open ourselves to God's boundless love, that love slowly and gently begins to change our lives. Although we may not understand this change while it is happening, our lives and our relationships continue to be reshaped, beyond our own designs, by an all-powerful and all-knowing Creator who understands us better than we can understand ourselves.

Once we begin to sense the changes God is generating in our lives, we also begin to experience "Faith...the realization of what is hoped for and evidence of things not seen" (Hebrews 11:1). We begin to experience faith in God's love.

If we are unable or unwilling to trust, perhaps because we fear any changes in our lives that we cannot imagine or control,

God waits patiently for us to open the gate. That is the nature of our relationship with God. An ever-present God loves us eternally. We, in exercising our free will, can choose, at any time, to receive or to avoid that love.

Inevitably, the extent of our willingness to trust God, to receive the gift of faith, and to welcome God's transforming love into our lives will influence the extent of our usefulness to God and, in turn, our own peace of mind and our personal sense of fulfillment. Without that trust, we become increasingly confined to living within the limits of our own judgments and finding satisfactions within the parameters of our own fears. We become, like Jonah, stuck in the belly of the whale.

~

As Joseph entered his third year at St. Albert's Seminary, his entire world was beginning to shatter. He was finding it increasingly difficult to continue, by the sheer force of his will, the strict, flawless observance of God's commandments which he had unreasonably demanded of himself. And though the path he was on was the path he had been taught to follow, the path the saints seemed to have followed, his resolve and his energy were beginning to deteriorate. Still Joseph remained willing to trust God unconditionally and to rely on his living faith in God's plan for him; and even through the long, despondent days and months ahead when he would come to doubt the very existence of God, God's abiding love continued to transform his life.

~

Afflicted now with an ever-deepening depression, Joseph went to bed each night praying for God's guidance, only to awake each morning to pray for the strength to make it through one more day. As he struggled through one distressing day after another, he found no one he felt he could talk to, no one he could trust enough to confide in, no one he could rely on to help him in his deep despair.

He was nearly seventeen and his doubts about himself had reached a deafening crescendo. His calling notwithstanding, Joseph had developed into a full-blown adolescent, grappling with all the conflicts that beset adolescents as they grope for their identity. Pulled every which way, first by hormones and then by holiness, first by presumptions and then by submissions, first by inflexibility and then by humility, Joseph began to compare himself and his choices to those of his peers.

Some of his siblings and his friends back home were already busy thinking about their futures, choosing colleges and careers and working at part-time jobs. In lighter moments, they were happily preoccupied with going to parties, hanging out together at local social halls and soda parlors, dancing, and dating. Most of all, they were rushing headlong into those exuberant, youthful scrapes that helped them to push the boundaries of acceptable behavior and define their own limitations.

Maybe, he pondered and wrestled with himself, he should be out there enjoying some of those happy adventures. Perhaps he was not really so different. Perhaps he was not really cut out for religious life. Perhaps celibacy was not one of his gifts. Perhaps, in time, he could be like everyone else. At least, he might find some comfort in blending in, and, maybe, if he made the right choices, some of his isolation and pain might go away. Maybe, he struggled to rationalize, God had meant for him to follow a more conventional path through life.

Some of his peers were already becoming engaged and planning to marry. This seemed a reasonable alternative. Joseph turned the idea over and over in his head: "Why don't I leave, just go home and get married," he would ask himself. "No, stay here; this is where you're supposed to be," his voice would answer back. And the next day and the next, the decision would have to be made all over again.

On those days when he felt most disillusioned and confused, he judged himself a failure, a person too distracted and too unworthy to be truly holy and pleasing to God. Perhaps his search for God was futile. Perhaps he should just follow along with the crowd. Perhaps the God he sought so passionately did not even exist.

Day in and day out, for the next three years, these conflicts continued to assault him, obscuring clarity and resolution. And day in and day out, for the next three years, he submitted himself to fulfilling his obligations without discernment and to facing his exhausting conflicts without another human soul to give him solace or advice. And though he ached for the presence of Jesus, he was still given no tangible replacement for the familiar and comforting companionship he had once enjoyed.

~

As Joseph was grappling with his identity and searching for his path through life, the world was grappling with the aftermath of World War II and the threats of a potentially more devastating Cold War with the Soviet Union. At Nuremberg, Germany, a ten-month trial concluded with twelve top-ranking Nazis being sentenced to death for crimes against humanity. Two years later, in 1948, an international tribunal in Tokyo would sentence former

Japanese Prime Minister Hideki Tojo to death.

Before the end of 1946, Winston Churchill would make a speech in Fulton, Missouri, alerting America to the dangers of Soviet aggression. For the first time, in that speech, he would identify the boundary lines drawn by the Soviet Communists around their satellites as the "Iron Curtain."

That same year, the United Nations would purchase a site for its international headquarters in New York City with an $8.5 million donation from John D. Rockefeller, Jr.; and Mother Frances Cabrini would become the first American citizen to be canonized by the Catholic Church.

By 1947, the Cold War between the United States and Soviet Russia had begun in earnest. The Soviets had broadened their control over Hungary and were politically advancing on Czechoslovakia. President Truman issued a doctrine advocating the principle of Soviet political and military containment. In retaliation, the Soviets accused the United States of being "war mongers" in the UN General Assembly.

Before the end of 1947, as a defense against the threat of Communist infiltration of the government, Truman would institute a loyalty program for civil servants to ensure internal security; and at Oak Ridge National Laboratory, scientists were beginning to research peaceful uses for atomic energy.

While record-breaking snowfalls caused eighty deaths in the North Atlantic states that winter, a debate over the separation of church and state was heating up when the U.S. Supreme Court upheld a state law permitting parochial school students to ride on public school buses.

Near the Dead Sea, in Wadi Qumran, one hundred scrolls dating from 22 BC to 100 AD were discovered. A year later, in

1948, Norbert Wiener would publish his breakthrough work, Cybernetics, and the computer age would be launched.

In 1977, some thirty years later, The Temple Scroll, the longest of the biblical texts that had been found near the Dead Sea, would be reproduced and distributed, using computer technology to decipher and catalog the text.

～

Although we were barely conscious of the implications of these post war events, we were hurtling toward inconceivable and bewildering changes in the way we viewed ourselves and our lives. Simultaneously building instruments of world peace and world destruction, we were on the brink of a social, political, and scientific revolution.

～

It was an equally startling and sweeping revolution that confronted an ancient society over two thousand years ago, a spiritual revolution that has proven to be timeless and that continues to reverberate through all our personal and social interactions. It was a revolution that eternally illuminates for us the path to a genuine and lasting peace.

At the Last Supper, Jesus promises: "Peace I leave with you; my peace I give to you. Not as the world gives do I give it to you" (John 14:27). This gift that differs from the peace "as the world gives...it" is an extraordinary kind of peace. It is the peace of Jesus. Not the apathetic, lifeless state of mind that we often call "peace," not the political and social structures of peace we try to build, this is a peace different from any peace we have ever known. It is a peace that echoes the original meaning of the word, from the Indo-European root, *pak*: to fasten or to bind,[9] as in a pact between two people or two nations. It is a peace that binds us to God and to His purpose in our lives.

In His instructions to His apostles, Jesus gives us an insight into the difficulties we will encounter on the path to this "peace...Not as the world gives"; and He warns that His presence will be like a sword, creating dissension, not peace, even between the closest family members:

> Do not think that I have come to bring peace upon the earth. I have come to bring not peace but the sword. For I have come to set a man against his father, a daughter against her mother, a daughter-in-law against her mother-in-law; and one's enemies will be those of his household.
>
> (Matthew 10:34-36)

Jesus goes on to explain that those who would follow Him must be willing to endure the cut of his sword, the loss and separation from anyone or anything that has become more important to them than Him:

> Whoever loves father or mother more than me is not worthy of me, and whoever loves son or daughter more than me is not worthy of me; and whoever does not take up his cross and follow after me is not worthy of me. Whoever finds his life will lose it, and whoever loses his life for my sake will find it.
>
> (Matthew 10:37-39)

Hardly an apathetic, carefree state of relaxation, the peace Jesus offers is found on a path paved with conflicts, with the loss of things familiar, and with personal suffering. On this path, we are invited to make a commitment, a binding agreement, to love no one more than Jesus, to let the sword of Jesus separate us from anyone or anything we love more than Him. We are invited to pick up our cross, to willingly accept responsibility for our lives, our strengths, and our weaknesses. And we are invited to follow Jesus in the direction that He is leading us.

This peace which we see in Jesus, His own peace which He promises us, springs from His pact with His Heavenly Father, a pact to bind His will to the will of His Heavenly Father. "I came in the name of my Father" (John 5:43), Jesus tells His accusers in Jerusalem. He continues to define his pact with His Father: "I cannot do anything on my own; I judge as I hear, and my judgment is just, because I do not seek my own will but the will of the one who sent me" (John 5:30).

When we accept the invitation Jesus offers us and make a decision to follow in His footsteps, we bind ourselves with Jesus in the pact He has made with His Father. We, too, make a commitment to bind our will to the will of God. And it is then, when we are living in harmony with God, when we have made a commitment to follow God's plan for us, that we experience the genuine, lasting peace Jesus promises.

~

In his last three years at St. Albert's, Joseph had come to know the sword of Jesus. In his commitment, his pact, to follow God's will as he discerned it and to stay faithful to his calling, he had been cut off from taking part in the healthy, vigorous socializing and explorations of adolescence. And although his parents and siblings fully supported him on this path, his chosen life in the institutional setting of the seminary also cut him off from the everyday comforts of his home and family. With his fervent spiritual yearnings, he was cut off even from his spiritual directors; and with his shy and sensitive personality and his zealous pursuit of perfection, he found himself cut off from many of his fellow seminarians.

Each day, as Joseph took another methodical step toward his goals, he took another step further away from all that was familiar and comforting in his young life. And he suffered separation and loss on a daily basis.

He was becoming increasingly resigned to the loss of his childhood companionship with Jesus. While he continued to find spiritual sustenance in receiving Communion, the emotional comfort he had always found in the daily liturgy was also slipping away; and his daily routines were becoming unbearable.

Soon his prayers turned into barren, repetitious sounds that seemed to fade into a cold, careless void. His confession of sins began to echo in his mind like a thousand noisy demons mocking his sincerity. His long hours of penance failed to quiet the echoes; and his meditations led him in circles, from desperate longing to deepening despondency.

Everything he had ever learned about keeping God's commandments, about rooting out his sins, and about perfecting his devotion to God, was crumbling inside him like the dry, brittle, discolored pages of some ancient book of laws.

Even his cherished desire for holiness began to crumble. His hair shirt, his hard bed and cold showers, his extreme acts of penance: all his calculated efforts to achieve spiritual perfection had betrayed him.

With an overwhelming sense of unworthiness and futility, Joseph acknowledged defeat. He would never achieve spiritual perfection; he would never be holy; he would never be a saint like the great saints who were his heroes. Bewildered by all he was losing, and exhausted by his struggles, he resigned himself to whatever destiny had in store for him.

The sword of Jesus had been sharp and swift, separating Joseph from anyone and anything that he might come to love more than Jesus himself. This separation, necessarily, had to include Joseph's single-minded, self-designed crusade for spiritual perfection and every self-conscious step he had ever taken to achieve that perfection.

As Jesus continued to lead Joseph toward God's purpose for him, Joseph was losing his entire life as he had come to know it. What sustained him in those years of loss, those years of jarring uncertainty and growing despair? And why did he continue on through a sea of self-doubts and bitter disappointments?

It was true, of course, that he admired his own tenacity and self-discipline, his ability to hang in there on his worst days, on the days when he could see no good reason for hanging in there. But tenacity, like self-discipline, is simply a muscle. By itself, neither tenacity nor self-discipline can sustain us through a prolonged and difficult commitment, nor can it nurture a human heart.

The French poet, mystic, and philosopher, Charles Péguy, describes hope as she who "who lies down every evening and gets up every morning."[10] Sometimes that's a huge act of trust – to persevere when we see no light at the end of the tunnel and to trust that God loves us as much, and perhaps more, in our weakness as in our strength.

For Joseph, his innate, living faith, alone, helped him to persevere; and his only anchor in the stormy seas of his adolescent despair was the hope not only that God would love him in his weakness but also that his life of faith would, in time, lead him back to his beloved Jesus. And he prayed that, in some inexplicable way, all he was suffering was part of God's plan for him.

So Joseph picked up his cross – his depression, his doubts, his faith, and his fervent yearning for God – and continued to follow in the footsteps of Jesus, on the path that Jesus intended for him, toward the peace that Jesus promised.

~

The year was 1949. In the U.S.S.R., a nuclear physicist, Igor V. Kurchatov, had just developed the first Soviet atomic bomb; and Germany had split into two republics, the German Democratic Republic in the East and the Federal Republic of Germany in the West.

In response to Soviet aggression, The North Atlantic Treaty Organization (NATO) was being formed to protect its Western allies from a Communist threat.

On mainland China, the Communist Chinese had defeated the Nationalists and had appointed Mao Tse-tung as the chairman of the newly established People's Republic of China, with Chou En-lai as premier and foreign minister. The Nationalists had fled to the island of Formosa where they were setting up a government under Chiang Kai-shek.

In America, eleven leaders of the U.S. Communist Party were convicted of conspiring to overthrow the government and sentenced to prison.

~

With the world careening so rapidly and so radically toward an unknown future, young and old alike were caught between a fascination with what was coming and a longing for what had passed. While Simone de Beauvoir was criticizing the historical role of women in her newly published feminist work, *The Second Sex,* the traditional role of women was being celebrated in a popular new musical, *Gentlemen Prefer Blonds,* featuring the hit song "Diamonds Are a Girl's Best Friend."

And in that same year, George Orwell was predicting a world in the grip of "Big Brother," in a totalitarian satire entitled *1984;* while Christmas, 1949, found everyone cheering the underdog – or the under reindeer, in this case – in Johnny Marks's whimsical tune, "Rudolph the Red-Nosed Reindeer."

We were a society looking back and moving forward, a society resisting change and envisioning revolution, a society on the threshold of startling breakthroughs and unthinkable potential for destruction.

~

Joseph Francis was completing his last year at St. Albert's Seminary, studying for the New York State Regents Examinations in his required subjects, and planning to begin his training at White Friars, the Carmelite seminary in Auburn, New York. He had proven himself a conscientious and capable student, with a rigorous course of study that included Latin and Ancient Greek, a full complement of modern languages, as well as comprehensive instruction in the grammar, usage, and etymology of the English language.

62

In addition to his linguistic skills, Joseph had developed a perceptive, penetrating, and curious intellect, and he was eager to begin studying the great writings that had influenced the Church and shaped the course of religious history.

While at St. Albert's, he had been left virtually on his own to explore the far reaches of his spiritual and intellectual curiosity. It was completely on his own that he examined the writings of St. John of the Cross and St. Teresa of Avila, writings his advisors had tried to discourage him from reading. As he pursued his interest, those writings proved to have significant spiritual value for him, and he was glad that he had not let himself be dissuaded from them. But, to his distress, he had no one to share his thoughts and his impressions with.

Now, he was eager to study the writings of these and other great saints with some of the leading Carmelite scholars of the day. He anticipated discussing his ideas with his instructors and with his peers, debating over fine points, and gaining new perspectives. While he entertained little hope that he would find spiritual companionship at White Friars, he did hold out hope that his intellectual isolation would soon be a part of the past.

Eighteen years old and desperately searching for a new understanding of his world, Joseph moved slowly and cautiously toward this next stage of his life. He had been disappointed many times before, and the depression he could barely endure was showing no signs of lifting.

~

During his years at St. Albert's, Joseph had been painfully and thoroughly stripped of his childhood approach to God, an approach based on the literal interpretation of God's commandments, an approach which he had been taught and which he had instinctively absorbed in his earliest exposure to religion, an approach that had, over the past five years, devastatingly betrayed him.

Now he was coming to realize that God's love for him was not based on his worthiness, or on his self-imposed suffering, or on some universally applied formula for eradicating his sins. He was coming to understand that God's grace was not given as a reward for meticulous adherence to religious dogma and protocol. And, as all his agonizing and exacting efforts were collapsing around him, Joseph was discovering that he could not force his way toward greater intimacy with God by impatiently and relentlessly demanding spiritual perfection of himself.

On the contrary, the more his desire for perfection deepened, the more intense his spiritual hunger grew; and the more intense his spiritual hunger grew, the more intangible God's presence became.

At times, he still experienced a longing for the Jesus of his childhood, but he had come to fully understand that he must go on without that much-cherished emotional comfort.

His innate, living faith, sorely tested under the daily pressures of his adolescent struggles, was now stronger than ever. And Joseph, stripped bare of all his preconceptions, submitted himself to waiting, as patiently as he could, for God to reveal Himself to him in a new and unforeseeable way.

Chapter Six

~

Into the Dark Night

*A little while and you will no longer see me, and
again a little while later and you will see me.*
(John 16:16)

On a glacial plateau in Upstate New York, on the road that winds
between Lake Cayuga and Lake Skaneateles, Auburn was one of
those grey towns that people would drive through on their way
to somewhere else. Here, Joseph Francis, now nineteen, entered
White Friars, the Carmelite seminary, where he would spend the
next three years of his life.

No longer the powerful, fiery, steam-spewing engine,
confidently speeding toward spiritual perfection, this novitiate felt
more like the clanking caboose, being dragged along the tracks
toward an unknown destination. His ordeal at St. Albert's had left
him feeling more vulnerable, more powerless, than ever before.
His mind and his heart had been scoured clean of every orthodox
lesson he had ever thought he learned, every religious principle
he ever thought he understood. And he did not know where he
could begin to look to find new answers. He could not even seem

to find the right questions.

In the past, Joseph had always been able to motivate himself with his quest for holiness, to reassure himself with his bold determination, and to fortify himself with his rigid adherence to Church laws. Now, his quest seemed futile; his determination, senseless; his rigidity, misguided. He felt foolish and ashamed. In those years when he had fought to humble himself, he had never felt so overwhelmed by humility as he did now. Not the untried, shallow attitude of humility that we put on when we go to church and take off when we get home, like an old coat, this was a true humility that he was gaining. This was the humility that we acquire, slowly and painfully, as we come to know ourselves.

And Joseph was coming to know himself as never before. He saw the youthful pride that had fueled his quest for perfection; he saw the introverted dreamer who believed in his dreams; and he saw the stubborn idealist who was unwilling to compromise his ideals. He saw his own fiercely independent and creative intellect, his deeply contemplative and acutely sensitive nature, and his painfully shy, apprehensive, and reserved personality.

Although he no longer was judging himself as right or wrong, good or bad, he wondered how a creature – such as he perceived himself to be – could possibly be pleasing to God.

In all the years that he had struggled to suppress his thoughts and control his body with acts of self-mortification, he had never suffered such an absolute and crushing mortification as he now suffered.

All his noble aspirations were negated by seeing how unforgiving and unrealistic he had been, impatiently demanding perfection from himself. All his extreme sacrifices became meaningless when he realized that he had been insensitive and judgmental toward himself, that his pursuit had been self-effacing and self-absorbed. And his preoccupation with becoming holy crumbled when he realized that he, Joseph, and not God, had determined the course he had followed.

Over the years, Joseph had labored painstakingly to expose his sins to himself and to God, but never before had his sins been as clearly and as abruptly exposed as they were now. He saw himself filled with mortal impulses, ego, willfulness, and arrogance. His youthful desire for holiness now seemed more like pride; and his commitment to the strict observance of the law now reminded him of the Pharisees.

How far off the mark he had landed! How far from his good intentions he had come! How very lost and confused he had been! The more he became aware of his predicament, the more vulnerable he became, and the darker the night that enveloped him. At times, when all he had come to understand about himself filled him with hopelessness and grief, he felt he might drown in the darkness.

And although God, unquestionably, was powerfully and lovingly present in that darkness all the time, perfectly molding and transforming the soul of the young novitiate to a deeper understanding of His will, Joseph found no solace. He was angry with himself for having been so mistaken about so many things. And he felt betrayed by God. He had always been willing to trust God, and, though he was misguided, he had faithfully struggled to earn God's love. Now, after so long and dedicated a search for God, he had never felt God so far removed from him, so far from his reach. If God had plans for him, God gave him no clue. If God was preparing him for some specific work, only God knew what that work might be.

And where exactly was God? Try as he might, he absolutely could not feel God's presence in that awful darkness. Had God utterly forsaken him because he had failed so miserably at being holy? Was God so disappointed with his spiritual confusions that He had lost patience with him? Was God playing some mean-spirited game of hide and seek with him?

And what did God want Joseph to do next? Where was the road map? Where were the new blueprints? Where was the new path?

If God did exist, Joseph had no idea where or how to find Him. And if God did not exist, Joseph had no idea where or how to go on with his life.

There simply seemed to be no answers to his desperate questions...only agonizing, persistent, dark silence.

$\sim$

It really did not seem to matter a whole lot at White Friars if you had doubts about the existence of the living God. The courses in Church history and Christian theology, even the studies in the Old Testament and the Gospels, had very little to do with the living spirit of God.

Although there are many powerful and inspiring exceptions, many theologians chose to concentrate, primarily, on the intellectual study of God and the relationship between God and the universe in a historical context. They examined religious doctrines and investigated matters of divinity. And reputable theologians, those with a doctorate in Sacred Theology, were permitted to raise questions regarding Church doctrines.

The existence and the spirit of the living God had little to do with the majority of the books that were written or with the doctrines that were taught. Many theologians simply examined the phenomenon of God in society, much as physicists examine the phenomenon of quarks in the universe. Rarely did personal belief in a living God or testament to the existence of a living God become part of the discussion.

Consequently, a student of theology could spend years inside the seminary walls and never once be called on to discuss the spirit of God or profess faith in the existence of the living God. That sort of thing was reserved for the chapel, and it was a personal issue between the student, his spiritual director, and God.

And that same student could spend those same years in seminary, in class after class, and learn nothing about Jesus, nothing about His life, nothing about His message, nothing about His compassion – and certainly nothing about His living presence among us.

~

Long months and years of studying Church history and theology did little to alleviate Joseph's anguish. If he was having trouble finding God in his life, he, most assuredly, was having trouble finding God in his classes. Sometimes, when he looked around the classroom and observed the expressions on the faces of his fellow seminarians, he wondered if they, too, were noticing what was missing.

~

Though painfully aware of exactly what was missing in those early years at White Friars, Joseph, nevertheless, welcomed the academic challenges and pursued his studies diligently. Besides satisfying his intellectual curiosity, his work often gave him the only relief he could find from the depression that continued to grip his mind and body.

With his keen imagination, Joseph was able to bring all the saints, and even some of the ancient theologians, to life; and he often enriched his own thirsting spirit with the wisdom of those great souls. Never a passive learner, Joseph was always fully engaged in every book he read; and every paper he wrote reflected his insightful intelligence and his heartfelt longing for God.

His earlier exposure at St. Albert's to the writings of St. Teresa of Avila and St. John of the Cross, although very important to him at the time, had only whet his appetite. Now there were no barriers to his continued study of their works. On the contrary, he was being encouraged to explore everything about these great mystics, to read and to ponder the words they had written, to explore their meanings, and to respond to their revelations.

He learned of earlier Carmelite writings, writings that had influenced St. Teresa and St. John, works like *The Institution of the First Monks* and the earliest Carmelite Rule that had officially defined Carmelite life. And he became acquainted with the writings of the French Carmelite, Saint Therese of Lisieux, who died in 1897, at the age of twenty-four, after a prolonged period of suffering with bouts of suicidal depression.

Each encounter with the works of these revered contemplatives opened yet another window inside his own contemplative nature and, even in his darkest hours, their mystical light penetrated to the deepest wellsprings of his soul.

To the list of Carmelites were added the writings of other great saints: St. Augustine, St. Dominic, St. Thomas Aquinas,

St. Francis of Assisi, St. Ignatius of Loyola, and some of the early Christian martyrs whom he had admired so much in his childhood. No longer simply his heroes, these saints now became human, men and women who had struggled, as he was now struggling, to find their way to God and to become transparent to God's purpose.

From each, he assimilated a different approach to God, an approach consistent with the experiences, the personality, and the nature of each saint. Yet beyond all their personal differences, he found a universal core. They all enjoyed an intimate relationship with Jesus and testified to His infinite love. They all dedicated their lives to obey God's will and to serve God's purpose. And they all embraced the unknown, considering God the source of all blessings, and relying solely on God's wisdom to guide them, God's mercy to protect them, and God's love to transform them.

~

In his lonely childhood years, Joseph had learned to rely on the gentle companionship of Jesus to give him solace. Now all that was left of that companionship was a warm memory.

As a fourteen-year-old seminarian, he was consumed by his relentless pursuit of holiness, and he relied completely on his strict observance of Church teachings to achieve that holiness. Now, he was stripped of all his adolescent illusions of controlling and directing his own spiritual path through life, stripped of his rigid formula for perfection.

More lonely and depressed than he had ever been, he found that he had fewer and fewer of his own emotional and spiritual resources to draw on. Drained and exhausted, he was forced to take each day as it came; and as one day passed into another, he slowly came to believe that an intangible and mysterious God

71

was guiding him along an unclear path, preparing his heart for a purpose he could not discern.

It was in the deepest anguish, the darkest nights, of those early adult years that Joseph Francis came to rely, solely, on a God he could not see, a God whose very existence often eluded him.

~

For his first three years at White Friars, Joseph's life was filled with the rigorous discipline of a seminarian in the throes of training and discovery, and the disciplines he had so intently developed at St. Albert's now served him well. Eager to learn as much as he could, his own curiosity frequently took over where the curriculum ended; and he often pursued his studies far beyond what was required of him.

He was especially eager to learn more about the history and the teachings of the Church, from its earliest beginnings with Jesus and Peter, through all the stages of its spiritual and political growth. The Church had always been an essential part of his spiritual life. When he was a child, the Church had been a daily sanctuary for him; as an adolescent, he had struggled with his own rigorous adherence to its teachings. Now, as a seminarian, he concentrated on the vital role of the Church in advancing Christian life; and he was dedicated to gaining a deeper understanding of its authority and to preserving its continuity.

His studies of the early Christian Church revealed the critical role the Church played in selecting the writings that were compiled in the Gospels. He gained new insight into the enormous responsibility of the Church to carry forth the mystical memory of Christ, to evolve through the gifts of the Holy Spirit, and to perpetuate the spirit of Christ, alive and responsive, down through the ages. And he explored the role of the priesthood, from its earliest days in the Church to the present.

Of all the paths that were opening for him as he advanced through his course of study at White Friars, he seemed to have the temperament and intellectual potential for serving the Church in some theological or diplomatic capacity.

~

The course of study for the priesthood ran through twelve months each year; and during the summer months, Joseph would attend classes at St. Bonaventure University, in Bonaventure, New York, and at Fordham University, in the Bronx. He would graduate from St. Bonaventure with his baccalaureate in the summer of 1953.

~

By 1952, the year before Joseph's graduation from St. Bonaventure University, the world's first hydrogen bomb had been successfully tested in America. Russia would detonate its first thermonuclear bomb a year later, in 1953, the same year in which Julius and Ethel Rosenberg would be executed for plotting to deliver classified U.S. military secrets to the Soviets.

The world was in a state of unprecedented peril, facing the scientifically documented and unthinkable threat of total nuclear destruction of all life on Earth; and its 2.3 billion people were being sorely challenged to hold on to any faith they may ever have had in the God of their understanding.

Little children, in every corner of the globe, were going to bed each night, looking out their windows at the stars, saying their prayers, and hoping that their world would still be there when they woke up the next morning. Although their parents had traditionally been their protectors, this generation of children was acutely aware that even their parents could not protect them from a disaster that would destroy the entire globe.

According to the United Nations statistics at that time, over 400 million of the world's 800 million children were going to bed hungry, as well as frightened, every night.

In a desperate attempt to respond to intolerable realities, some people were busy building underground bomb shelters in their homes and communities and stocking the shelters with canned foods and bottled water. Others joined rallies to protest the development of nuclear weapons; while at Brookhaven National Laboratories on Long Island, research into the development of nuclear power plants and other peaceful applications of nuclear energy was moving full speed ahead.

On July 27, 1953, a cease fire was signed, ending the Korean War; U.N. and U.S. forces headed home; and Communist North Korea remained divided from South Korea at the thirty-eighth parallel. Two years later in Vietnam, the Communist Viet Minh would defeat the French at the Battle of Dienbienphu, and Vietnam would also be divided into two parts, with the Communists controlling the North.

As if we were not traumatized enough by the threat of nuclear war and the potential of total annihilation, Rachel Carson's 1951 best seller, *The Sea Around Us,* had alarmed and alerted an oblivious nation to the widespread pollution that was contaminating the world's oceans and rivers and lakes, and poisoning the fish, the birds, and the wildlife that depended on those waters for survival.

Disillusioned with the direction in which society was

headed, groups of young people expressed their discontent by rebelling against conventional behavior. Their clothes, their speech, their music, their literature, and their choices set them apart from the mainstream. They were members of the "beat" generation, and their spokesman was Jack Kerouac.

The spiritual malaise of that time was also being reflected in the "theatre of the absurd," and Samuel Beckett's widely popular play, *Waiting for Godot,* dramatically represented the world's growing skepticism about the existence of the living God. Meanwhile, in the laboratory, the chemical basis of life was being decoded by James D. Watson, with his discovery of the double-helix structure of DNA; George Gamow, the Soviet physicist, in his book, *Creation of the Universe,* proposed the "big bang" theory of creation; and across the nation, Americans began reporting sightings of unidentified flying objects in the night skies.

During the daytime, Americans were glued to their black and white television screens listening to the Senate Subcommittee Hearings investigating instances of alleged Communism in government and the military. Senator Joseph R. McCarthy headed the combative investigation which, eventually, extended its arms into all areas of American life. Playwright Arthur Miller and Broadway actor Zero Mostel would be among McCarthy's unsuspecting, blacklisted targets, and their professional and personal lives would be profoundly affected. "McCarthyism" became a new term used to describe any abusive, unfounded, and sensational approach to political indictments.

By 1953, there were no longer any guarantees of safety anywhere in the world, not even in America; and every institution, from the family to the government, was in a state of inescapable upheaval. And there would be no going back!

~

In the Vatican that year, Eugenio Pacelli, Pope Pius XII, was in the fourteenth year of his nineteen-year reign. Three years earlier, in 1950, the National Council of the Churches of Christ had been established in America, with a membership of thirty-two million. By 1959, membership in the council would triple to nearly 110 million, bringing together twenty-five Protestant and four Eastern Orthodox groups. The Roman Catholic Church did not encourage its members to participate.

~

Joseph Francis was twenty-three years old, and only two years away from ordination. Now pursuing his studies at Whitefriars Hall, the Carmelite seminary in Washington, D.C., he was fast gaining a reputation as a brilliant speculative thinker whose deep mystical insights sometimes proved difficult even for his professors to comprehend.

During his years in seminary, Joseph had discovered that his philosophical pursuits provided a satisfying and comfortable haven for his contemplative and shy nature; and he wondered whether he might be suited for academic or diplomatic work in the Vatican on completion of his theological training. He was especially intrigued, therefore, when one of his professors recognized his unique abilities and suggested that he might be able to help Joseph secure a position in Rome as a speculative theologian.

Although Joseph felt comfortable with the prospect of working in Rome, he certainly might have guessed that God would have a less predictable plan in mind. Joseph had learned that lesson all too well during those frustrating and painful years he spent at St. Albert's in search of sainthood. And he also knew from experience, and from his unrelenting and long-lingering depression, that a predictable and comfortable haven was rarely the medium that God usually chose for the growth of his soul.

So it was not entirely surprising to him when nothing further was said about an appointment to Rome; and, even after his professor was reassigned to Rome as Superior General, Joseph, obedient to God's unfolding plan, decided to let the matter drop. In his book, *Never Alone,* he explains this pivotal career decision: "I had reached the point in my spiritual life where I had decided that I would place myself completely in God's hands and never scheme for the things I wanted."[11]

~

In 1955, after eleven years as a seminarian, Joseph Francis Girzone was ordained as a Carmelite priest and was sent out into the world to minister to God's people.

~

The world the young priest entered was in the throes of catastrophic social and political tensions. In Montgomery, Alabama, African-Americans were boycotting segregated public bus companies, and Dr. Martin Luther King, Jr., advocating a strategy of passive resistance, was leading a movement against segregation throughout the country. That same year, the Supreme Court ordered the immediate racial desegregation of all the nation's public schools. A year later, congressmen in the South would ask the states to resist the Supreme Court ruling by whatever legal means they had at their disposal.

Meanwhile, the Cold War had generated a stockpile of four thousand atomic bombs in the United States and one thousand in the Soviet Union, more than enough to destroy everything on Earth many times over. In reaction to the NATO alliance, the Soviets had formed the Warsaw Pact, which included Albania, Bulgaria, Czechoslovakia, East Germany, Hungary, Poland, Rumania, and the Union of Soviet Socialist Republics. And Communism came closer to our shores than we had ever thought possible when Fidel Castro landed in Cuba with his guerrillas in 1956 to attack the island's dictator, Fulgencio Batista.

For the children, in these frightening times, there was the arrival of Kermit the Frog, the first in a long string of Jim Henson's Muppets, to be followed shortly by Dr. Seuss's first two classics, *The Cat in the Hat* and *The Grinch that Stole Christmas*. For the adults, there was Thomas Merton's *No Man Is an Island*, Patrick Dennis's *Auntie Mame,* and the Broadway musical *My Fair Lady.* And for the teenagers, there was Elvis Presley.

~

By 1956, the General Conference of the United Methodist Church had approved full clergy rights for women; and in Stamford, Connecticut, Wallace Harrison was working on a modern architectural design for a new First Presbyterian Church. It would be the first church in the world to be built in the shape of a fish.

In Rome, the Vatican was only two years away from the election of Pope John XXIII. Within months after his election, the Holy Father would call for the opening of Vatican Council II, the first Vatican Council to be called in almost a hundred years.

~

What tools could this introspective, philosophical, reserved, and sensitive young Carmelite priest possibly bring to a world in the midst of such upheaval? He seemed entirely ill-suited, by temperament, by intellect, and by training, for the challenge.

What books had he read, what papers had he written that would give him insight into the fears, the alienation, the pain, and confusions of the people he would be sent to serve? He had received no training at all in understanding and attending to human psychology. Nor had he received adequate training to guide people through the process of spiritual growth.

And what theology could he rely on to help heal and direct the people who would look to him for comfort and hope? In all the years in seminary, he had found only limited healing for his own interminable depression and doubts in the body of knowledge he had accumulated. His studies in the Old Testament and the Gospels and the writings of the saints had been only marginally helpful to him in his own process of spiritual growth. How, indeed, could he expect to heal or direct anyone else?

Still, this young priest was extraordinarily well prepared for the work he was being called to do. Every day in Joseph's childhood, when he would turn to a warm and loving Jesus for companionship, God was preparing him to understand loneliness and to bring the love of Jesus to those he was about to serve.

Every day in Joseph's adolescence, when he would mercilessly drive himself to achieve perfection, God was preparing him to recognize human suffering, to identify human pride, and to be compassionate toward human frailty. And God was preparing

79

him to understand the inadequacy of Church law, alone, to guide the human heart and transform the human soul.

Every day in Joseph's young adult years, when he would search for God in the darkness, when his willingness to trust unconditionally and his innate and living faith was all he had, God was preparing him to understand human loss, to testify to the mystery of God's presence, and to offer hope that God would guide and heal those who believed in Him. He was being prepared to testify that God was the ultimate source of all gifts we receive: all joy, all loss, all grace.

In truth, God had been preparing Joseph to do His work before Joseph was born, before he had eyes that could see or ears that could hear (Mark 8:18). And God had blessed Joseph's life with an innate, living faith, the legacy of his mother's *fiat* to give him life, a faith so deep and enduring that it sustained him through all the years God was preparing him, one uniquely designed lesson at a time, to be His priest.

Chapter Seven

~

Faith under Fire

How narrow the gate and constricted the road that
leads to life. And those who find it are few.
(Matthew 7:14)

While Joseph was considering immersing himself in theological studies and writing, God was working on a different plan. That plan was to send this scholarly young priest out into the world as it was – a world being redefined daily, a world in the turmoil of loss and transition, a world desperately searching for answers. Here his years of training in theology would come alive; here his research would be informed by human struggles; and here his words would touch human hearts.

So Father Joe, obediently and willingly, accepted his first assignment.

Although he remained quite puzzled and uncertain about the direction in which God was pointing him, he balanced his misgivings with a staunch, unquestioning faith that had been steadily tested and strengthened throughout his years as a seminarian. Now in his twenty-fifth year, the young priest had already endured bitter loneliness, crushing disappointments, immeasurable losses, and an unforgiving and unrelenting depression. Through it all, and especially when God seemed the furthest from him, his faith deepened and matured. He remained open to receiving God's love and guidance; and that love and guidance continued to transform him.

Father Joe had already begun to notice some changes in himself, especially in the way he was responding to people and to circumstances. He found himself placing more and more decisions in God's capable hands; and the more he relied on God, the more he seemed to be set free from many of the misconceptions and distractions that had plagued his youth. He felt a little less alienated and lonely, a little less discouraged when his plans did not work out, a little less bewildered when he could not see the road ahead. And as he continued to let go of his own expectations and embrace God's plan for him, even his chronic depression began to disappear. Like his faith, Father Joe was becoming steadily stronger.

In the years to come, Father Joe's faith would be tested, again and again, in new ways, in ways he could not have anticipated; and the challenges he would face would arise not only from the hidden places within his own soul but also from the hidden places within the world. Joining Jesus in His ministry and entering the world as a servant of God, he would be directly confronted by forces, consciously and unconsciously, antagonistic to God. In time, he would come upon those forces everywhere – even in the Church, itself.

~

Father Joe's first day on the job was a nightmare. He had

been assigned to a high school that was directed by the Carmelites in the Bronx. Once a peaceful farm community on the outskirts of New York City, this northernmost borough, in the 1940s, had watched the rich topsoil of the Fuellner Farm being scooped up and transported to the Parkchester housing development for landfill. By 1955, when Father Joe arrived, the Bronx had been completely reshaped by a storm of social and economic changes, and the community was trying its best to cope with its overwhelming urban problems.

Father Joe found the house where he would be living with the other staff priests easily enough. The door was open, and when he went in, he found the house empty. Apparently, no one had arranged to welcome him or to help him get settled. Not knowing which room would be his, he waited around for several hours. Finally, a priest who was visiting at the school came through the door. As a visitor, he had no idea what Joseph's room assignment would be; but, that morning, he had overheard the older priests talking about someone named Joseph Girzone who would be arriving later in the day. The visitor told Father Joe that the priests seemed very distressed about his arrival and very upset that he had been assigned to their school.

While that explanation seemed to shed some light on the situation, it would be many weeks before Father Joe would understand why they had so totally, and so uncharitably, rejected his being there before they had even met him.

When one of the staff priests eventually did show up to direct Father Joe to his room, he was curt and cold, speaking in monosyllabic grunts and avoiding eye contact with the new arrival. His fellow priests were no more courteous, and as Father Joe met each one of them over the next few days, he was both hurt and confounded by their behavior toward him. Nevertheless, he tried to disregard their rejection as best he could and conscientiously applied himself to his duties at the school.

The young people he was assigned to work with were part of the post-war generation in America, the generation whose parents had come home victorious from World War II and who were now unable to protect themselves or their children from the rising threat of Communism and nuclear holocaust. This was the generation that had grown up watching *Father Knows Best* on the family's new ten-inch television screen and listening to the melodies of Eddie Fisher, a disillusioned generation that was now turning to street gangs for social structure and gyrating to the discordant rhythms of rock 'n roll for entertainment.

Father Joe knew something about being disillusioned and bewildered, and as a young priest, he was not about to forget the pain and anguish he had suffered during his own adolescence. When he listened to his students, many of them gang members themselves, he heard echoes of his own distress; and when he responded to them, it was with the compassion and understanding he had gained through his own struggles. And he had something even more powerful to offer these troubled street-wise teenagers. He had his unyielding faith in God's love. Whenever the timing seemed right, Father Joe would take the opportunity to talk to them about Jesus and to encourage them to receive the healing power of Christ into their lives.

Wherever he could, Father Joe reached out to the parents as well, trying to help them understand the gap that kept widening between the world they had known and the world in which their children were growing up. Often finding the parents in as much turmoil as their children, he ministered to their fears, their guilts, and their confusions. He often would share some of his own experiences to illuminate a point, and he always encouraged them to trust in the protection of God's love.

While the older priests continued to shut Father Joe out, he continued to keep his focus on his growing commitment to the adolescents and families in his charge.

For a young priest with so contemplative a nature and such scholarly aspirations, Father Joe had a remarkably gentle, relaxed, and down-to-earth manner that put everyone at ease. And although he was always honest and straightforward, he was never judgmental. People were openly drawn to him and liked to be in his company.

He soon discovered that he was a good minister and an especially good listener, and that the young people and their parents were responding positively to his sensitivity to their problems and his genuine concern for their progress. Steadily, he was able to build a comfortable rapport and a strong bond of trust with them, and he was becoming very well liked by both the students and the faculty at the school.

In time, as his effectiveness with these difficult and defiant teenagers became increasingly apparent, the priests, who had been so blatantly insensitive and rude toward him, began to show some signs of acceptance; and, in time, Father Joe learned why they had been treating him so badly. In *Never Alone,* he elaborates:

> ...there were problems in the school, many of the kids were on parole, and they had asked the provincial superior for a strong, muscular priest who weight-lifted, and when they got me instead, a skinny hundred-forty pound shadow, they resented it.[12]

A thought quietly flashed through Father Joe's mind when he finally learned the truth behind the icy initial reception he had received: "What if Christ had arrived at their door? How would the priests have greeted Him?"

~

Father Joe remained at the high school for four years, gaining valuable insight into the harsh realities that the families and youngsters in this urban environment had to face on a daily basis. He saw their struggles and sensed their heartfelt appreciation of his concern for them. And he saw how God was able to use him to bring comfort and hope into the lives of those he worked with. Most of all, he experienced the miracle of bringing Christ into a world filled with suffering and fear.

~

During those same years that a young Father Joe was attending to the spiritual and emotional crises of gang members on the streets of the Bronx, Leonard Bernstein and Stephen Sondheim were romanticizing gang life in a new, sell-out Broadway musical called *West Side Story.* A modern parallel to Shakespeare's *Romeo and Juliet,* the play foreshadowed the epidemic of violence and tragedy that would soon mark the lives of America's urban youth.

~

Far from the growing brutality and violence of the city streets, Father Joe's next assignment would also take him away from the rich cultural and social life of New York City which he had come to enjoy. In stark contrast, he would find himself surrounded by the physical and emotional impoverishment of a bleak coal-mining town in Pennsylvania. There he counseled the hard-working, weary coal miners and their families, befriending them and bringing what light he could into their darkened lives.

It was a difficult assignment for a young priest, and, at times, Father Joe felt himself inadequate and ineffective in bringing them the comfort and relief they so badly needed. Some were suffering with chronic illnesses and disabilities from their years in the mines; others struggled with alcoholism; and everywhere and always, the memory of previous mine disasters and the threat of new disasters hung in the air.

Their suffering seemed constant, and though he could respond with compassion and understanding, he could not change the circumstances of their lives. They even seemed to receive the sacraments as just another habitual routine in a life they had come to accept. At times, the young priest became more distressed by the circumstances he encountered than were the people he was trying to comfort; and he often anguished over the their deep, relentless wounds.

Yet, in many ways, this assignment proved to be a haven for Father Joe. Here, he found himself surrounded by simple people with strong traditional values and beliefs, people with modest expectations living in the kind of close-knit, homogeneous community that was becoming rare. Here people welcomed every chance they had to enjoy a family birthday or a holiday or to help a neighbor; and here, through generations of hardship, people had learned to rely on themselves, on each other, and on their prayers to see them through. Here, in this small Pennsylvania coal-mining town, time seemed to stand still, as if it were disconnected from a world that was moving faster every hour, a world that was growing smaller every day, a world where empires were collapsing and morals and manners were eroding.

~

Precipitated by the Cold War and by extraordinary advances in technology, our understanding of life, itself, was being redefined. In the years since Father Joe had been ordained, America had entered the race for space against the Soviet Union. Beating us to the punch, the Russians launched the first man-made satellite, *Sputnik I*, in 1957, to be followed, that same year, by *Sputnik II*, with Laika, the first dog in space, aboard.

America retaliated with the formation of the National Aeronautics and Space Administration and an all-out push by the Office of Education to bring the scientific curriculum in our schools up to the standards set by the Soviets.

By 1958, the year the Soviets launched *Sputnik III*, America successfully launched its first satellite, *Explorer I,* to be followed, later in that year, by *Vanguard I.* One year later the Soviets would land *Luna 2* on the moon, and then launch *Luna 3,* which would photograph the dark side of the moon.

Having lost the first two rounds of the race to the Soviets, America set its sights on becoming the first nation to send a man into space. But, again, we were too late. Yuri Gagarin, a Soviet cosmonaut, earned the title of "The First Man in Space," aboard the Soviet-made *Vostok 1*, months before Project Mercury could launch Alan Shepard in *Freedom 7*.

It was now 1961, and Americans were reeling from this blow to their national pride. In the coming years, Americans would suffer many such blows.

Back on Planet Earth, Pan American World Airways had

already begun offering regularly scheduled transatlantic jet flights to Europe; and John Glenn had set a new transcontinental speed record flying a *F8U-1P* jet aircraft from Long Beach, California, to Brooklyn, New York, in 3 hours, 23 minutes, and 8.4 seconds.

In England, a replica of *Mayflower II* was built; and, commanded by Alan Villiers, it made the ocean voyage from England to Plymouth, Massachusetts, in fifty-three days. The original Pilgrim voyage, in 1620, had taken sixty-seven days, a full fourteen days longer.

Speed just for the sake of speed was fast becoming a universal obsession.

As people were moving more rapidly toward their destinations and toward each other, the information they generated was being more rapidly communicated than ever before in history. By 1957, a bionic computer that could print, write, and respond to verbal directions had been introduced; and, a year later, Xerox produced its first commercial copying machine. In Europe, one hundred and sixty electronic computers were already up and running; in America, the figure was over one thousand.

By 1959, nearly 150 million American families had television sets in their homes. That same year, *Explorer VI* would send back television pictures of the Earth from outer space; and all of us on Earth would have a brand new perspective of our place in the universe.

At the same time that new frontiers were being explored in outer space, old empires were falling apart all over the globe. By the end of 1962, the struggle for national independence had swept through most of the world like a tidal wave; and England and France, and all the other empire builders in Europe, had surrendered their hold over the majority of their former colonies. As if swept away in the undertow of this tidal wave of independence, the code of manners and morals, that once seemed to define our behavior for generations, disappeared. In their place, nothing but the manners of the moment remained.

In America, a thirty-year-old ban for obscenity was lifted, opening the way for the publication of D. H. Lawrence's *Lady Chatterley's Lover* and Henry Miller's two novels, *Tropic of Cancer* and *Tropic of Capricorn.* Italian film director Federico Fellini depicted the breakdown of behavioral codes in the sexually explicit *La Dolce Vita,* and directors Ingmar Bergman and Francois Truffaut followed with films of unprecedented realism. Andy Warhol painted a widely acclaimed "pop art" portrait of a can of Campbell's soup; and "junk" sculpture became the newest form of artistic expression.

On the Broadway musical stage, Rodgers and Hammerstein's *The Sound of Music* reminded us of the power of love to bridge the gaps between the past and the present, and Lerner and Loewe's *Camelot* transported us, for a few pleasant hours, to simpler times and simpler values. But when we left the theatre, we returned to a hi-tech world we could only barely comprehend.

RNA and DNA, the genetic building blocks of life, had just been synthetically created in a laboratory; and the biological creation of life could now be controlled with a tiny white pill that was being sold to women for the first time. The National Radio Astronomy Observatory in West Virginia had started listening for radio signals from intelligent beings on other planets. And over eleven thousand scientists had petitioned the United Nations to end nuclear weapons testing, claiming that current levels of radiation on Earth would cause five million cases of birth defects and cancer over the next one thousand years.

By 1963, Washington and Moscow would be connected by a private telephone wire. This "hot line" would give the United States and the Soviet Union immediate contact with each other in case either nation accidentally launched a nuclear warhead.

~

In a single decade, between 1950 and 1960, America's churches had expanded their membership with fifteen million new parishioners, the largest numbers joining the Roman Catholic Church, the Southern Baptist Convention, the Churches of Christ, and the Methodist Church. In Sweden, in 1960, for the first time in its history, the Lutheran Church ordained three women. By the end of the next decade, women would be ordained in both the Episcopal and the Anglican Church; and the first American woman would be ordained as a rabbi.

In 1960, America elected its first Roman Catholic president. At forty-three years of age, John Fitzgerald Kennedy was also the youngest man ever to hold that office. Three years later, on November 22, 1963, in Dallas, Texas, an assassin's bullet would end his life; and a nation in shock would publicly mourn their loss.

~

Faithfully responding to the spiritual needs of a changing world, and committed to promoting Christian unity, Vatican Council II began the first of its four annual sessions in early October 1962. It was now three years since newly elected Pope John XXIII had first called for the Council; and all over the world, in every religion and culture, all eyes were expectantly focused on Rome.

Although most of the final documents would not be issued until the fall of 1966, live interviews and reports of the proceedings were steadily circulated through the media; and debates on the implications of this historic event were heating up long before anyone had a clear understanding of the outcome. What was absolutely clear to everyone was that the posture and the tone of the Roman Catholic Church, as the world had come to know it, was about to be transformed beyond our imagination.

A month after the first session ended, Pope John XXIII issued his famous encyclical, *Pacem in Terris*. It was a powerful and compelling document, a papal effort to stop the escalating conflicts of the Cold War and restore peace; and people everywhere, searching for a visionary, spiritual leader who would heal and unite an anxious and polarized world, began to regard Pope John XXIII as that leader.

Six months later, on June 3, 1963, a bulletin, issued from the Vatican, plunged a world that was just beginning to dare to hope into despair and mourning. Pope John XXIII had passed away.

It would now be up to Pope Paul VI to carry on the work that had been started.

~

While the Vatican Council was vigorously at work in Rome, Father Joe continued in his ministry. After Pennsylvania, he had been assigned to teach in the seminary and, then, in other schools directed by the Carmelites; and everywhere he was stationed, he was surrounded by a stream of bewildering rumors that were trickling out of the Vatican and filtering through his world.

He was now thirty-three years old, and, like so many of

us, he felt himself caught in the crosscurrents of a fast-fading past and an undetermined future that we seemed to be in the process of destroying.

And, like so many of us, he had been encouraged and inspired by the dynamic vision of Pope John XXIII, by his active commitment to a new world of unity and peace and his sacred commitment to the spiritual evolution of the Church. Father Joe would never forget those commitments, and, in years to come, they would continue to reverberate in his own dreams for a more harmonious world and a more embracing, universal Church.

~

During the twelve years that he had spent in seminary at St. Albert's and, then, at White Friars, Father Joe's social and academic environment had been culturally and spiritually one dimensional. The theology he studied excluded any extensive training in the foundations of other religions; and almost every person he came to know was Roman Catholic, with some ethnic variety, here and there. Much like the Church, itself, he had been disconnected and discouraged from experiencing the spiritual and cultural differences that were an essential part of the human fabric.

It was not until he was a young priest, assigned to work in the Bronx, that he had been exposed to people from all walks of life and began to develop easy relationships with people from all religious and ethnic backgrounds. He became fascinated with the rich cultural tapestry of the neighborhoods where he worked; and he admired the simple pleasures that people found in preserving and sharing their unique heritage and beliefs. Jews and Lutherans, Episcopalians and Methodists, he soon counted them all among his friends, and they respected and valued his friendship in return.

While cultural differences geographically divided people in the Bronx into separate, clearly defined, ethnic neighborhoods, with nothing more than a street sign to mark their boundaries, Father Joe had discovered that their suffering, their joys, and their dreams crossed those boundaries indiscriminately. He also discovered that he had crossed those boundaries indiscriminately; and that, in truth, his caring and compassion for the people he knew and worked with in those neighborhoods knew no boundaries.

In some mysterious way, his assignments in the Bronx had thrust this parochially trained priest into the middle of the world as it was, and, although he still entertained hopes of studying and writing some day, he truly had enjoyed being there.

~

In December 1965, Vatican Council II completed its mission. The body of constitutions it had generated was collected into several volumes and became part of the official Canon of the Church. It would take many years for the full impact of the reforms to be felt in the local parishes, and bishops' conferences all over the world were convened to interpret and implement the new vision of the Church. In America, alone, the changes would affect close to forty-five million Catholic parishioners.

While the Catholic bishops poured over the official documents, and the laity waited curiously to see what would happen, theologians, in every denomination, eagerly seized the opportunity to study and analyze, to expound and debate, and, generally, to add to the vast body of literature that was being built up around this critical turning point in Church history.

Before long, Roman Catholic churches all over the world began to look different and to sound different. Latin, as the official language of the Church, was almost immediately replaced by each country's native tongue; and for many worshippers, it was the first time in their lives that they were able to fully understand and participate in the liturgy. For others, this fundamental change symbolized the end of the Church's centuries-old cultural and spiritual heritage, a heritage that was inextricably tied to the cadences of the Latin language.

Many churches began to dismantle their sacred works of art, their paintings and statues, and others replaced the traditional Crucifix with a more modern, impressionistic Cross. Slowly, church by church, the railing in front of the Altar was removed, and worshippers were no longer asked to kneel and receive Communion from the hand of a priest. Church by church, the Altar, itself, was moved forward and priests were now facing their parishioners when they celebrated the Mass.

For the first time in centuries, people were being encouraged to read the Bible, especially the Psalms, and to increase their understanding of the liturgy as their primary source of spiritual nourishment. They were being invited to participate in the Mass as Eucharistic ministers and to be part of a Church community that was responsive to their unique spiritual needs.

The universal call to holiness that came out of Vatican Council II was a clear mandate for the Church to relinquish its hierarchical dominion over God's graces and to open its doors to every parishioner who was seeking a personal encounter with God. What all this meant to the parishioners, at that time, differed from one person to another. For some it meant a welcome, long overdue change; for others, it was a devastating loss of familiar and comfortable habits of worship; and worse, some felt they were losing the very way in which they had come to view themselves in relation to their Church, in relation to their priest, and in relation to their immortal souls. While many lapsed Catholics returned to the new Church, some totally rejected the changes and walked away. In America, alone, at the time of the Vatican reforms, over twenty percent of the population were members of the Catholic Church.

For everyone, inside or outside the Catholic faith, the work of Vatican Council II offered continued hope that Pope John XXIII's vision of Christian unity and world peace was still alive.

～

Father Joe had been assigned to serve as a pastor in the Albany diocese the year before the work of Vatican II was completed. In many ways, this new assignment was a homecoming for him. He was now back in the area where he had grown up, not far from the Church where he had been baptized and confirmed and where, at the age of two, he had first become attracted to the priesthood. It was here that he decided to enter the seminary and to dedicate himself to becoming a saint. And after his ordination, it was here that he returned to be with his family whenever he had free time in his schedule.

Still, it was a strange homecoming; and he seemed to be the stranger. He sensed how much he had changed since his boyhood in Albany. Then, a lonelier and more literal Joseph had fortified himself with a zealous drive and an official blueprint for spiritual perfection. Now, he had no grand schemes, no burning ambitions. Although he did hope to be able to study and write someday, his only real ambition, since his ordination, had been to serve God and to serve God's people. And the more he brought God's peace and love into the world, the more his own restlessness and anxiety evaporated. For the first time since he could remember, he began to experience true joy. So, Father Joe eagerly went wherever he was sent, eagerly served as he was led to serve, and eagerly grew in the ways God planned for him to grow.

And, clearly, he had grown, in ways he could not have imagined, in ways only a loving God could have arranged. He now perceived all of God's world as one creation, not separated by race, religion, or ethnicity. His sensitivity to the endless suffering in the world had heightened, and his desire to reach out with compassion to that suffering had deepened. He had become acutely conscious of the excruciating wounds that Jesus endured, wounds he saw everywhere he went; and he prayed for the grace to help heal those wounds.

In the Albany diocese, the same year that the Vatican Council finished its ground-breaking work, clergy and laity, alike, struggled to build a new Church. Many of the clergy, like the parishioners, were uncomfortable with the radical changes, while others eagerly embraced them.

The religious had their own challenges to face; and while some were delighted with their new freedom, eager to take off their traditional habits, to reform their orders, and to expand their ministry further into the world, others preferred to maintain their traditions and to cling to the old ways. Still others, deeply disturbed by the upheaval, left religious life.

In truth, the reforms that had come out of Rome were reverberating throughout the world and, especially, throughout the Catholic Church. At its most dynamic level, Vatican Council II had challenged everyone to redefine their calling, renew their commitment, and rethink their path to salvation.

With everyone reacting every which way to the new Church, it was not an easy time to be a parish priest; but it was a time of great opportunity. For the first time in hundreds of years, people were actively engaged in searching for answers. And for the first time in hundreds of years, they were able to approach their clergy and seek assistance in that search. No longer a part of an unapproachable, hierarchical elite, post-Vatican priests were expected to relinquish their tightly held authority over the activities in the Church and to view their parishioners as participants in a Christian community.

For Father Joe the opportunity was particularly welcome. He had never nurtured career ambitions within the hierarchy of the Church; and, as a leader, he had always believed that true authority was derived from interaction with others, never from controlling the actions of others. So, the reforms posed no threat to his perception of himself as a priest within the Catholic Church. As a servant of God and a minister to God's people, he embraced the call to make the Church more responsive to the needs of the community, and, in his own heart, he extended that community far beyond the borders of his parish.

During the nearly twenty years that he served in the Albany area, Father Joe did, in fact, extend his ministry into the outlying community. He continued to teach, served on local civic boards, and earned a reputation as an impartial, evenhanded mediator. The chairman of a human rights commission, he was instrumental in helping to settle prison riots and in easing racial tensions in the school system. And he was an advocate for the forgotten, for aged prisoners in jail, for the poor in his parish, for troubled children everywhere. Whenever there was a need in his community, he made himself available, and the community, gratefully, accepted his help.

As his parishioners grew in the new spirit of the Church, Father Joe encouraged and supported their efforts to reach into the larger community and, in whatever way the spirit prompted them, to contribute to generating peace and unity in the world. They soon were opening their doors to the Jewish community and to other Christian churches, organizing ecumenical prayer services, and working together to support important social programs for the children and for the poor.

The parishioners brought all their unique gifts together to help improve their community and their Church. In truth, they were the Church; and dedicated to their purpose, they were able to bring peace and harmony and unity to their small corner of the globe.

~

During the Sixties and Seventies in America, peace had become the exception in a society of unprecedented violence. The Sixties, alone, saw the assassination of four of the nation's most prominent political and social leaders. In 1963, the same year that president Kennedy was assassinated, an assassin's bullet took the life of the NAACP Field Secretary, Medgar Evers. Four years later, civil rights leader, Dr. Martin Luther King, would be assassinated, and that same year, a Jordanian Arab, Sirhan Bishara Sirhan, would fatally shoot Robert Kennedy, the younger brother of the assassinated president.

Six days of looting and rioting in the Watts district of Los Angeles in the mid-Sixties marked the beginning of more than a decade of unrest in the nation's urban ghettoes. In the years to follow, riots would break out in cities across the country, followed by weeks of violent crime, burning buildings, and lootings. In city after city, the National Guard would be called in to restore a fragile peace, as the ghettoes of Chicago, Cleveland, Detroit, Newark, and New Haven turned into battlefields of racial conflict. The rioting reached into the Attica State Penitentiary in New York, where state troopers and police had to be called in to put down the uprising and free the thirty-eight guards held as hostages by the inmates. By the Eighties, the tension would spill over into places like Miami, Florida. There, race riots would claim the lives of eighteen people and cause over a hundred million dollars in property damage.

~

In 1962, one year before the assassination of President Kennedy, the United States Supreme Court had ruled that reciting prayers in public schools was a violation of the First Amendment of the Constitution. A decade later, over half the high school students surveyed indicated that they had used one form of illegal drugs or another. Thirty percent were still using marijuana.

~

On the nation's university campuses, militant students held disruptive protest rallies and revolted against school and government policies. Anti-war sentiments first expressed in Pete Seeger's 1961 folk melody, "Where Have All the Flowers Gone," found new expression in demonstrations and rallies, aimed specifically against America's military involvement in Vietnam; and in the Haight-Ashbury district of San Francisco, thousands of "hippies" came together for an antiwar "love in," fueled by the folk music of social protest, careless sex, and illegal drugs, including the hallucinogen LSD.

In the decade of the Sixties, alone, violent crime in America had escalated fifty-seven percent.

And violence was erupting across the globe: in Northern Ireland between the Catholics and the Protestants; in the Middle East between the Arabs and the Israelis; and in Iran between the Shah and the Islamic fundamentalists, under the leadership of Ayatollah Khomeini. At the Olympic games in Munich, Germany, in 1972, Arab terrorists killed two Israeli athletes; and in 1976, Palestinian terrorists hijacked an Air France plane at the Entebbe Airport in Uganda, provoking an Israeli commando raid to free the hostages.

Meanwhile, the civilized world, in reaction to the overpowering and uncontrollable chaos and violence that was erupting everywhere, turned to a passionate pursuit of peace. By the end of the Seventies, some twenty million Americans were finding hope and inspiration in transcendental meditation, yoga, mysticism, Buddhism, and the charismatic movement.

In 1967, at Duquesne University in Pittsburg, Pennsylvania, a group of people came together, on retreat, to pray for a greater presence of the Holy Spirit in their lives. The group had met before and a few had reported receiving the gift of tongues at a prayer meeting organized by a member of the Presbyterian community. At the Duquesne retreat, many of the participants reported an immersion in the Spirit, and still others manifested the gift of tongues for the first time.

The Charismatic Renewal movement in the Catholic Church was born at that meeting and, within a few years, charismatic prayer groups and preparatory Life in the Spirit seminars became part of the spiritual life of many parishioners.

Encouraging an intensely personalized experience of the Holy Spirit, Charismatic Renewal presented a sharp contrast to more traditional formalized worship and contemplative prayer. While many hailed the outpouring of spiritual gifts that characterized the new movement, others were opposed to what they felt was a highly emotional, self-willed experience.

Unintentionally, in its own unique way, the charismatic movement had contributed, dramatically, to the tensions that were already growing inside the Church.

~

Experts in the development of human organizations will usually agree that "necessary tension" is a crucial ingredient for the vitality and growth of an organization. Certainly, the Catholic Church proved that point. In the years following the Vatican reforms, "necessary tension" was the order of the day. Bishops were disagreeing with other bishops – and with their archbishops; priests were disagreeing with each other – and with their bishops; and parishioners were disagreeing with everyone. Some of the most conservative parishioners, uncomfortable with all the confusion, even expressed anger at Pope John XXIII who started the whole thing. Anyone from the outside looking in probably wondered how the Church was managing to hold together at all.

On the inside, the "necessary tension" often reached a distressing pitch. While everyone was trying their best to be faithful to the spirit of the reforms, many in the Church, both in the hierarchy and in the laity, were influenced by entrenched attitudes and emotions that did not easily melt away. And in many instances, there was an unbridgeable gap between the generations.

While most younger members of the Church were enthusiastically forging ahead, many older members felt confused and betrayed.

Father Joe was thirty-two years old when the Vatican Council met for its first session. Long before, in his late teens and through his years in seminary, he had become disillusioned with the harsh, rigid laws of the Church he had grown up in. Supported by his faith in God, and by God's guidance in his life, he had remained obedient to the teachings of that Church and steadfast in his calling to the priesthood; but he was increasingly aware that the spirit of the Church had been buried under the dogma.

In his early years as a young priest, his awareness often translated into frustration, a gnawing dissatisfaction with his own limited ability to provide comfort to people and to bring "the good news" into their lives. Although people were drawn to his quiet faith and his genuine concern for them, they were often so preoccupied with their sins, their guilts, their feelings of inadequacy, and their fears that they built barriers between themselves and God. And a young Father Joe too often felt powerless to help them remove those barriers.

Now, through the gifts of the Holy Spirit, the Church was transforming, removing many of the rigid legal barriers they had erected between their parishioners and God. There was a new spirit of freedom in the Church; and priests could be more open with their parishioners, revealing new sources of spiritual nourishment to them, helping them discern God's guidance in their lives, and encouraging them to be active participants in their own spiritual growth, as well as in the spiritual well-being of their Church.

Not every priest and not every parishioner was

comfortable with that new freedom. For many parishioners, freedom implied an unwelcome share of responsibility for their own salvation, and the end of a passive dependency on their Church. For many of the clergy, it represented a devastating breakdown in the hierarchy, a perceived loss of authority and control over the spiritual gifts of the Church and the salvation of the flock. In truth, a good number of the clergy, schooled and seasoned in the pre-Vatican Church, were personally uncomfortable with the accessibility, the responsiveness, and the interaction with parishioners that this new freedom generated.

For Father Joe, the new spirit of freedom was a divine grace, an open window through which God's love could enter people's hearts and heal their lives. This spirit invoked in him a sacred responsibility to help people remove any barriers, within themselves or within the Church, which kept them from receiving God's love. For Father Joe, the new spirit of freedom was an answer to prayer.

As parishioners slowly began to redefine their relationship to God and to the Church, Father Joe facilitated their spiritual renewal and encouraged them to trust themselves and to be open to God's guidance in their lives. If they were tormented by their sins, he guided them toward a forgiving God. If they felt unworthy of God's love, he reminded them that God's love was unconditional. If they were filled with guilt and shame, he assured them that God would never abandon them.

And he did everything possible to ensure that the Church reflected the spirit of a forgiving, loving, ever-present God. Time and again, he illuminated Church doctrine in the light of each parishioner's unique spiritual needs; and, at all costs, he protected his flock from injustice, no matter where that injustice originated.

In August 1978, Pope John Paul I succeeded Paul VI. He served for thirty-three days. Upon his untimely death, John Paul II was elected to the papacy. Now nearly twenty years since Pope John XXIII had first called for Vatican Council II, a full spectrum of reactions to the Council's reforms could still be found inside the Church. Most of those who had resisted the radical changes initially continued to do so. Others, who had embraced the reforms, implemented them liberally in order to meet the rapidly changing needs of their parishioners. Still others proposed even more profound, far-reaching reforms. For everyone, no matter what their stance, those twenty years were charged with stressful disagreements and mounting challenges.

For Father Joe, the post-Vatican years were as stressful and challenging as for anyone else – and more so. His unwavering commitment to minister to the spiritual needs of his flock often put him at odds with some of his fellow priests and, at times, even with his superiors. When he discerned that it was necessary to allow a divorced parishioner to receive Communion, he risked confrontation. When he opposed a parish fund drive that was clearly beyond the means of his poor parishioners, he risked appearing disobedient. When he chose obedience to God over obedience to hierarchical authority, he risked attack.

Year after year, the struggle between the fading laws of the old Church and the living spirit of the emerging Church made the present a time of exasperating conflicts. But it was precisely the "necessary tension" created by that pulling and tugging, that action and reaction, that contributed to making the Church more vital and dynamic than it had been in centuries. The Church had come alive, and the laity and the clergy, interacting with each other and with the Holy Spirit, promised to keep it alive.

~

In 1981, Father Joe received an alarming call from his doctor. Now fifty-one years old, he had noticed that he was tiring too quickly, becoming irritable too easily, and getting headaches too frequently. Brought up in a family that, from the time of his conception, attached little significance to a doctor's advice, he was not in the habit of thinking about his health. But, this time, his symptoms were interfering with his work, and he decided to check things out.

The results were more distressing than he could ever have imagined, and the doctor was adamant.

"If you want to be alive at the end of this week, you had better get into my office right now," he warned.

"This sounds like it could be something really serious," Father Joe quipped, trying to lighten the mood.

"It is!" the doctor snapped back. "It is very serious!"

Before the day was over, Father Joe was in the doctor's office listening to the grave details of his condition. His blood pressure had reached dangerous levels, and if he hoped to avoid a stroke, he would have to find some way to lower that pressure. Medication, alone, would not do the job. He would have to slow down his active pace of life. The doctor strongly recommended that he consider retiring if he wanted to stay alive.

What a blow! How could he retire at such an early age? It seemed he had so much more work to do. There were so many people who were still suffering, still wounded, without joy, frightened, and alienated from God's healing love. There was no way that he could consider retiring.

On the other hand, how useful would he be if he had a

stroke, if he were paralyzed, or, worse, if he died?

He would have to retire, and he would have to find another way to do his work.

But first, he would have to deal with the immediate concerns of tying up his affairs. He would have to speak with his parishioners and his long-time colleagues in the diocese. And he would have to speak with his bishop. He and his bishop did not always see eye to eye, and he could not be sure how the news of his needing to retire at such a young age would be received. He could only hope that the bishop would understand his medical crisis and accept his decision to retire, but if he didn't, there would be mounting conflict and tensions.

The doctor had warned Father Joe that he could not tolerate any stress at all, that he was flirting with death, and that he could not afford to ignore the seriousness of his condition. So Father Joe made another critical decision. He would offer to retire without his pension. The diocese was always concerned about their budget, he reflected, and his retirement would probably be a lot more acceptable to his bishop if he relinquished his pension. Of course, he had no idea how he would make a living, how he would survive. But that was a problem for another day. His first priority was to take himself out of harm's way.

And he did. With the same kind of raw courage and deeply rooted faith that his mother had relied on to save his life before he was born, Father Joe resigned. The bishop accepted his resignation and gave him no argument about his offer to retire without his well-earned pension. Father Joe remained a priest in good standing in the Church; and, for the time being, he had reduced his stress enough to live at least one more day.

~

What a long, winding road he had traveled, so far from anything he had ever planned or imagined. What an adventure he had been on, and how oddly and abruptly it was coming to an end. He had learned so much, matured so much in his understanding of human nature and his understanding of the Church. He had been to places and met people and done things he could never have hoped to do when he graduated from the seminary. All he ever considered doing, then, was studying and writing, perhaps in Rome. Instead, he had spent twenty-six years as a teacher and minister in schools and parishes, working with teenage street gangs and parents and coal miners and rioting prisoners and politicians. He had watched the Church he loved go through radical changes and evolve, and he had faithfully done what he could to contribute to that evolution.

Now he was uncertain about his health; he was without a job; and there were days, with no money in his pocket, that he was without any food as well. On good days, he could afford to buy a frozen dinner at the supermarket and cut it into three portions, one portion for each meal of the day. On other days, he had to rely solely on God to nourish him. And God never abandoned him.

In *Never Alone*, he writes of those days:

> For the first time in my life I was nearly penniless. I had just enough to survive. I ate food many poor people would turn down. I had no money for clothes. I made my furniture from some boards I bought cheap. I had one plate, a bowl, a couple of glasses, and three

utensils. I knew for the first time in my life what it was to be genuinely "poor," in the world's sense of the word. But these were the happiest days of my life....I had to practice what Jesus taught and what I had preached all my life, "Look at the birds of the air...."

One morning, I was taking a walk, and wondering what I would do for supper, since I had no money. Walking along the side of the road I thought I saw some money in a ditch. But how would money get into that ditch so far from anyplace? I took a closer look and bent down and sure enough, there, lying in the ditch and neatly folded, was some money, just enough for supper. I could almost hear Jesus saying, "I told you not to worry, I would take care of you." Jesus was right and I could now say that from my own firsthand experience.[13]

~

A lonely young boy had traveled a lifetime with Jesus: attracted to His gentle companionship in his childhood; seeking to be holy and pleasing to Jesus in his early adolescence; and suffering the abysmal loss of His discernible presence throughout his years in seminary. Now after joining Jesus in the world, after faithfully strengthening His Church and ministering to His people for twenty-six years, Father Joe was completely alone. And his abiding, living faith in his beloved Jesus was there to sustain him.

Chapter Eight

~

The Joshua Years

*I say to you, no one can see the kingdom of God
without being born from above.*
(John 3:3)

Face to face with his own mortality, Father Joe began to think about
his life, about his trials and his blessings, and, especially, about his
relationship with Jesus. Ever since his days in seminary, he had
searched for a deeper intimacy with Jesus. He had relinquished his
own expectations and inclinations to follow faithfully wherever
He led him. Father Joe had been His shepherd, a minister, and an
advocate for His sheep; and he had been His priest and helped
to build His Church. Over the years, Father Joe came to love all
God's children as part of one flock; but in the deepest chambers
of his soul, there was no love greater than his love for Jesus. Now,
as he faced this latest trial, he sensed that his lifelong relationship
with Jesus was about to transform again and that he would come
to know Him in an entirely new way.

So many times in his youth and in his years as a priest,
Father Joe had relied on God's love to emotionally and spiritually

sustain and guide him; and though he would often find himself confused and anxious, God, in His own time, would quiet his fears and illuminate his path. Now, through physical and economic conditions that seemed totally beyond his control, he found himself as dependent on God's love and mercy as he had been before the dawn of his own consciousness, before his own endangered birth. Now, fully conscious, he was all too aware that his life had come full circle and that, once again, his very survival was in God's hands.

As he looked back on all his earlier struggles – his loneliness, his losses, his depression, his disappointments – he also realized that God had never challenged him beyond his ability to grow; and each trial he had faced had helped him to mature in an understanding of God's ways and in a devotion to God's purpose. Likewise, he realized that his God-given blessings – his abiding attraction to God, his enduring faith, his compassionate and contemplative nature – all these helped him to stay open to God's abundant love, to renew his trust, and to strengthen his resolve to do God's will. Now, as he confronted this newest crisis, he sensed that he was about to face even greater challenges and that he was about to receive even more unimaginable blessings.

Still, from the outside looking in, there appeared to be no logic in the direction his life had taken. When he had desired perfect holiness, he had been purged of that desire and had been led to discover his very ordinary humanity; when he had considered immersing himself in abstract theology, he had found himself immersed, instead, in the harsh, naked realities of life. And now, after years of obediently accepting God's plan for him, he seemed to be left with no apparent plan at all.

All he really seemed to have left was a dream, a vision not

yet completely formed, yet a vision that lingered right under the surface of his consciousness, a vision of "the good shepherd... (who) lays down his life for the sheep" (John 10:11-16). It was a vision that had been informing his every response as a priest, a vision that had been fueling his passion for serving the needs of his parishioners, a vision that, consistently and intuitively, had been molding his perception of Jesus and His Church.

During his twenty-six years as a teacher and parish priest, Father Joe had come to see the Church as a sanctuary, a safe place where the good shepherd would gently and wisely care for the flock and offer his life for them. Instead, he all too often found his parishioners being chastised and persecuted by rigid laws that alienated them from the experience of God's healing and transforming love. Even the reforms of Vatican II only seemed to highlight an ongoing, underlying struggle within the Church – one he had faced throughout his life – a struggle between the strict adherence to the laws of the institution and the compassionate, embracing ministry of the good shepherd.

As Father Joe had been growing in his relationship with Jesus and in his own ministry, his vision of the good shepherd had been growing. At all times, he had tried his best to be a good shepherd to his flock, to treat God's children as part of one flock, and to lead them toward the healing and compassionate arms of Jesus. And wherever possible, he tried to ensure that the law did not divert God's children from the joy and freedom of a personal relationship with Jesus or discourage them from seeking refuge in His loving, outstretched arms. If only he could make his emerging vision of the good shepherd a reality for more people, people of every religion and nationality, people who Father Joe knew were suffering, people who he sensed were joyless and hungry for

God's universal, healing love.

Perhaps now would be the time for that vision to take shape. Perhaps that was the reason God had so abruptly shifted the course of his life and had made him so totally dependent on His love. Perhaps this was the reason he was being challenged, as never before, to welcome God's abundant love into every corner of his life and to let God love him as only God was able to love him. Perhaps, as before, God was preparing Father Joe to serve some unique creative purpose that God had planned for his life.

~

Challenged by the Pharisees to identify the greatest commandment, Jesus responded: "You shall love the Lord, your God, with all your heart, with all your soul, and with all your mind. This is the greatest and the first commandment. The second is like it: You shall love your neighbor as yourself. The whole law and the prophets depend on these two commandments" (Matthew 22:36-40).

And at the Last Supper, Jesus, who had rested all Jewish law on two simple acts of love, addressed the apostles, saying: "I give you a new commandment: love one another. As I have loved you, so you also should love one another" (John 13:34). How very important it must have been to Jesus that we love one another as He loved us, important enough, in fact, to add a new commandment to the law.

Of these three commandments, the new commandment Jesus gives us often proves to be the most difficult for us to fulfill; for it is the only commandment that implies that we welcome God into our lives and receive from God His abundant and all-encompassing love. When we try, we usually can find ways to love our God with all our hearts, all our souls, and all our minds. We do all this, of course, in our limited human way, sometimes giving our hearts and souls and minds to distractions, to other gods, for a while, then turning back to God each time our false gods disappoint and betray us. And God accepts our vacillations, our struggles, and our love.

We usually can also find ways to love our neighbors as ourselves. This is not so very difficult. When we treat ourselves with self-acceptance and self-respect, the love we give our neighbors will be compassionate and respectful. When, on the other hand, we treat ourselves in a self-centered or self-effacing way, the love we give our neighbors will likewise suffer.

So responding to the first two commandments seems within the reach of our human ability. Not so with the new commandment Jesus gives us. For how is it at all possible for us to love one another as Jesus loves us? We are not God! We are not Jesus! We rarely can find it in our hearts to love others without conditions, without expectations, without imposing our own agenda on a relationship. And rarely do we feel confident and caring enough to offer others unguarded empathy and mercy and boundless compassion.

How is it possible, then, to be so converted that we, ourselves, can love as Jesus loves? That is a challenge of a very different nature! And it is a challenge that can only be met when we choose, of our own free will, to open our hearts and welcome the transforming love of Jesus into every corner of our lives.

Only by continually receiving His ever-present and boundless love into our lives, and continually allowing that love to work in our souls to convert us, can we personally come to experience and understand the way Jesus loves us. Only then can we begin to grow beyond the boundaries of our limited, self-defined concept of love and begin to love one another as Jesus loves us.

This new commandment, then, asks that we do more than simply give our love to one another: it asks, first, that, day by day, we receive the transforming love which Jesus gives us; and, then, day by day, that we turn around and offer that love to others. And as Jesus is always available and eager to love us, to slowly and gently prepare us, through His love, to love one another as He loves us, all we have to do is be willing to say "yes" and receive His transforming love in our lives.

The only problem we may face with this new commandment, then, seems to come from our own reluctance to receive the love Jesus offers. When we resist opening ourselves to being loved by Jesus, unconditionally and compassionately, in the way only Jesus can love us, we remain ignorant of His love, unwilling to be converted by His love, and, consequently, unable to love others as He loves us. We remain incapable of fulfilling His new commandment.

Nor is it surprising that we may be reluctant to receive the love Jesus offers us. His love can shock us, just as bright light can shock a person who was once blind. His boundless love can illuminate our limited lives and our limited approach to love; and what we come to see in the light of His love can often hurt our eyes and our hearts. The light of His love can penetrate to our dark places, showing us our own shortcomings and the shortcomings of our relationships with others. In contrast to the way He loves us, so much of what we have come to accept as satisfying can begin to appear superficial, self-serving, and unsatisfying.

So we often choose to avoid the love Jesus offers us,

staying in the dim light of our own making, keeping everything in its place, not rocking the boat on which we sail through life. Alienating ourselves from our full potential to receive and give love, we alienate ourselves, as well, from our full potential for intimacy and freedom.

It is only when we are willing to continually open our hearts to the love Jesus offers us, and are born again in the spirit of His love, that we can begin to experience the transformation that only His love can offer. And as we are transformed by His love, one small miracle at a time, we begin to build the capacity to love one another as He loves us.

For most of us that willingness comes only under duress, in times of stress and calamity, when we are forced to rely totally on His boundless love, accepting Jesus into every corner of our lives. Opening ourselves totally to His love, we slowly come to find ourselves at peace, and we learn not to be afraid. We begin to experience the true, original meaning of the word "freedom," from the Indo-European root *prai*: precious, beloved, at peace.[14] We begin to find ourselves loving one another as Jesus loves us. And we begin to fulfill the new commandment that Jesus gave us.

～

In 1975, six years before he was forced to retire, while still working in the Albany diocese, Father Joe had tried his hand at writing. His first book, *Kara,* was a short fable that told the story of a lonely falcon who is transformed, in a moment of compassion, from a predator to an empathetic protector of the small birds and rodents in the forest where he lives. Once transformed, Kara is no longer motivated to kill for his food; and although he has no idea how he will survive, he soon finds himself nourished by the love he receives from his new friends, by the spiritual nourishment he receives from God, and by his growing attraction to God's light. The book, which was self-published, sold over 25,000 copies. Although simple in its story line, Kara reflected the profound contemplative nature of its author and his deep faith in the power of God's love.

Now physically weakened and unsure, himself, of how he would survive, Father Joe turned to writing once again. And he wrote about what he knew best. From his lonely childhood and adolescence, and from his many years working with young people – counseling members of street gangs, teaching biology in the Carmelite and parish schools, and college Latin in seminary – Father Joe was well acquainted with the struggles of teenagers. In *Gloria: A Diary,* he explores these struggles, as a young teenage girl tries to learn about herself and discover her place in the world that surrounds her.

Alone with her deepest hurts and fears, Gloria finds she has no one to confide in, not her parents, not even her closest friends. In her loneliness, she turns to God; and her diary records her growing relationship with God and with Father Angelo, who introduces her to Jesus for the first time. A good shepherd, Father Angelo is able to offer Gloria the human warmth and understanding she needs as she begins to heal her emotional and physical wounds. For the blossoming teenager, who was never particularly religious, the friendship she builds with Father Angelo becomes her first living experience of genuine Christian love, the love of one person for another, love as Jesus loves us.

Gloria, which was also self-published in 1982, was followed that same year by *Who Will Teach Me?: A Handbook for Parents.* In it, Father Joe focuses on the challenges parents face in teaching their children about Christian life. Addressing many difficult issues, including sin, sex, heaven, hell, death, and the Church, Father Joe called on his vast experience as a priest and upon the insights he had gleaned from his own childhood in a conservative Catholic family. Filled with his vision of the good shepherd, he encourages parents to help their children build a personal relationship with Jesus, a relationship that will help their children develop compassion, self-esteem, and acceptance of themselves and others.

About sin, he writes in *Who Will Teach Me?:*

Teaching right from wrong has to be a well-thought-out process and should be integrated into the child's friendship with Jesus. So parents might consider that children not be taught about sin until they have been taught about Jesus and have begun to express good feelings about Jesus. Once the child does this, the parent can then begin to relate the child's own behavior to Jesus. For example, the parents have already taught the child how kind Jesus is. So when the child is doing something mean or unkind, the parent takes the child aside and reminds her of Jesus and of her friendship with Jesus. The child is told that if she is a friend of Jesus, she will want to be like Jesus and will be kind to people. It works, believe me! And it doesn't give the child a bad feeling of having broken a commandment that is punishable by God's justice.[15]

Over and over again, as Father Joe wrote one book and then another, a single message was emerging: The key to resolving the majority of our dilemmas – as individuals, as communities, and as societies – could be found in a dynamic, personal relationship with a compassionate Jesus, in the boundless love of "the good shepherd," gently and purposefully at work, transforming our lives and changing the nature of our interactions with one another.

~

By 1981, the year Father Joe was forced by critical health problems to retire from parish administration, relinquishing his pension to avoid conflict with his bishop, a major economic boom was beginning to sweep through the nation. Fueled by "trickle-down Reaganomics," as well as by an on-going infusion of foreign money from oil-rich Arabs and industry-rich Japanese, the Eighties would soon be characterized by a continuation of the excessive inflation that had begun in the Seventies and by excessive personal and government spending. The "me" generation, described by Christopher Lasch in his 1979 study *The Culture of Narcissism*, would evolve into a generation of "Yuppies," young, upwardly mobile, and acquisitive.[16] In reality, some of the extreme affluence generated in the Eighties would "trickle down" to the rest of society, but, in retrospect, it would become clear that the "new rich" were not using their vast resources to build and strengthen the foundations of personal and social wealth. Instead, extravagantly spending their money on non-durable goods and services that quenched their thirst for immediate personal gratification, they would enjoy a pleasurable, but short-lived, day in the sun.

Meanwhile, posing a stark contrast to the excesses of the day, Mother Teresa began drawing worldwide attention to her work among the sick and the poor. A rare example of selfless compassion, she was awarded the Nobel Peace Prize in 1979.

Beset by conflicting values and global and technological upheavals, the world was ricocheting from one extreme to the other. The search for meaning lured over nine hundred people to Jonestown, Guyana, in 1978, where they died in acts of mass murder and suicide at The People's Temple. In 1981, while the Chinese Communists were easing their restraints on religious freedom and allowing many of their Buddhist, Muslim, and Christian churches to reopen, an assassination attempt was made on the life of Pope John Paul II. The finger of blame was pointed at Muslim extremists.

Earlier, in the spring of 1979, in the *Église Saint Germain* in St. Germain-en-Laye, a quiet medieval town outside of Paris, the Youth Mass commemorated the recent signing of a peace treaty between Egyptian President Sadat and Israeli Prime Minister Begin. The Mass, celebrated in French, was filled with hope and was strikingly punctuated by the Youth Chorus singing "Hatikvah," the national anthem of Israel, in Hebrew. Two years later, in 1981, Anwar Sadat was assassinated by fundamental Muslim extremists in his own country.

That same year, advances in American medical technology led to the first successful prenatal surgery performed on an unborn infant; and in 1982, the first successful artificial heart implant opened yet another door to the extension of human life.

While some technologies were promising to improve human life, other technologies were seriously threatening to destroy it. At the Three Mile Island nuclear plant near Middletown, Pennsylvania, damage that had been detected in 1979 continued to forebode a major catastrophe; and in 1980, at Love Canal in Niagara Falls, New York, where toxic chemical wastes had hazardously contaminated the entire region, a state of emergency was declared.

Six years later, in 1986, in Chernobyl, Russia, an explosion in a nuclear plant would bring death and incalculable danger into the lives of over five million people in the immediate range of the blast; and winds carrying radioactive dust would destroy livestock as far away as Scotland and northern Wales. Health officials throughout Europe, attempting to evaluate the damage to the food chain, would lower the standards for radioactivity in milk and milk products, grains, and fish; and within the next ten years, incidents of cancer, at every age level, would be reported to have risen over sixty percent throughout Europe and over six hundred percent in Chernobyl.

As the millennium loomed closer and closer, many people began viewing these disasters – along with the global outbreak of AIDS, record-breaking earthquakes and hurricanes, and an unmitigated rise in social violence – as irrefutable signs that the world was reaching the end times.

Still others, pointing to the Harmonic Conversion of 1987, claimed the approach of a new era of unparalleled peace.

Addressing contemporary peace movements and contemporary violence, Thomas Merton had written in *Conjectures of a Guilty Bystander:*

> There is a pervasive form of contemporary violence
> to which the idealist, fighting for peace by nonviolent
> means, most easily succumbs – activism and overwork.
> The rush and pressure of modern life...are a form,
> perhaps, of the most common form of its innate
> violence. To allow oneself to be carried away by a

multitude of conflicting concerns, to surrender to too
many demands, to commit oneself to too many projects,
to help everyone, is to succumb to violence. More
than that, it is cooperation in violence. The frenzy of
the activist neutralizes their work for peace. It destroys
their own inner capacity for peace. It destroys the
fruitfulness of their work because it kills the inner
wisdom which makes their work fruitful.[17]

~

Forced by the circumstances of his health to remove
himself from any and all arenas of contemporary violence, Father
Joe was challenged, as never before, to let God into every corner
of his life, to let God love him and work in him. He was challenged,
as never before, to be rather than to do. He was challenged to let
God do for him more than he could ever have imagined doing
for himself. And the more he let God love him and work in him,
the more freedom he experienced, freedom from fear, freedom
from doubt, and freedom to follow his own deepest intuitive
promptings.

Those promptings had led him to write *Kara* and *Gloria*
and *Who Will Teach Me?* They were also leading him back to
the Gospels, once again, and to many of the original writings
of the early fathers of the Church. And they were leading him
back to that time in human history when Jesus walked the earth,
proclaiming God's love and promising the kingdom of heaven to
all who followed Him. As he poured over the writings of the early
Church fathers, Father Joe was struck by the purity and intensity
of their love for Jesus and their unwavering faith in His promise of
heaven. Motivated solely by that love and that faith, they endured

unbearable suffering with hope and joy. The foundation of the early Church was the inspired Word of God, and the early Church could be found wherever people came together to share their faith in that Word.

Only a few centuries later, under the Emperor Constantine, Christianity was proclaimed an official state religion. From that time on, the Church became enmeshed in the political hierarchy of the day; and the spontaneous sharing of faith gradually gave way to religious coercion, legalism, armed conflict, and earthly power. As Rome began to crumble under the invasion of Germanic tribes, the pope organized an army to protect the Roman people. Grateful for the help the Church provided, the Roman people gave vast sums of money and land to the Vatican.

By the time of the Reformation, many powerful Christians had also initiated a practice of offering money and land to their bishops in exchange for the promise of salvation. Paradoxically, at the same time, the Roman Catholic Church was embarking on its own brand of reform, establishing the Inquisition to seek out and persecute heretics. Whether motivated by political or religious passions, the efforts of reformers and inquisitors, alike, gradually turned the focus of religious institutions more toward their formal and theological differences than toward their spiritual and historical unity in Christ. And the dynamic impact and mystical memory of the man Jesus, as well as the universal community of the early Christian Church, slipped further and further into the far recesses of our consciousness.

As Father Joe immersed himself in the history of the Christian Church, he anguished over all that had been lost following the reign of Constantine. Lost was the simple sharing of faith in the inspired Word that defined the early Church. Lost was the spontaneity and joy of Christians of every nationality coming together as one people in God. Lost was the personal sense of the man Jesus who had touched so many lives with His love and who had changed the course of human history with His promise of heaven. Lost was the vitality and reassurance of the Word made flesh.

All these thoughts stirred in Father Joe's heart and mind as he continued his studies of the Gospels and the early Church fathers. How could what was lost be recaptured, restored, and revitalized? How could we find our way back to the dynamic, personal experience of Jesus and to the joyful, universal faith of the early Church? A world made increasingly smaller by technology, yet splintered into hundreds of conflicting pieces, seemed to be crying out for such unity, crying out for a renewed sense of universal truth.

~

In his Homily at Boston Common, Massachusetts, in 1979, Pope John Paul II spoke of the importance of receiving God's love:

> Faced with problems and disappointment, many people will try to escape from their responsibility, escape in selfishness, escape in sexual pleasure, escape in drugs, escape in violence, escape in indifference and cynical attitudes. But today, I propose to you the option of love, which is opposite of escape. If you really accept that love from Christ, it will lead you to God.[18]

For Father Joe, unconditionally receiving the grace of "that love from Christ" in those years of extreme poverty and critically poor health did, indeed, expand his soul and lead him closer to God. And as he continued to absorb the message of the Gospels, "that love from Christ" led him, as well, to a profound spiritual renewal, to a new sense of Jesus.

As if seeing Jesus for the first time in his life, Father Joe marveled that an entirely different Jesus jumped off the pages of the Gospels; he saw the son of God being truly human and mingling with just ordinary human beings. Always aware of the mystical divinity of Jesus and the compassion of the good shepherd, Father Joe was now discovering the engaging human nature of the man Jesus. And what he was discovering was a robust, forthright, and good-natured man who was comfortable with Himself and comfortable with people from all walks of life – tax collectors, prostitutes, lepers, fishermen, entrepreneurs, children; a man who paid no heed to social or religious hierarchy; a man who claimed no authority, except that which flowed from His obedience to God's will and revealed itself in His loving service to God's children.

And thousands of people from all walks of life were comfortable with Him, for He accepted and loved them as they were. He enjoyed their company and openly shared in their laughter as well as their sorrow. And he neither took offence nor was resentful or critical when people mistreated Him. Rather, He was sensitive to their shortcomings and had a profound understanding of the suffering that often precipitated their behavior.

If this man Jesus seemed harsh toward anyone it was toward the Pharisees, the religious leaders of the day, men totally dedicated to keeping the letter of God's law with little concern for the spirit of that law. These men he admonished, calling them "fools "(Luke 11:40) and "hypocrites" (Matthew 23:13). And in the Parable of the Pharisee and the Publican, Jesus again reflected his position on the law, clearly teaching us that the humility and true repentance of a sinner carried far more weight with God than the methodical observance of the law by a proud and self-righteous religious leader.

As the humanity of Jesus continued to unfold in his awareness, Father Joe faithfully continued to explore that humanity and to delve more deeply into the message of Jesus. Time and again, he discovered that Jesus ridiculed laws and regulations that had nothing to do with man's relationship with God. And time and again, he discovered that Jesus always put the needs of the people before the dictates of the law. The role Jesus modeled for religious leaders was as minister to God's children, healing their hurts, lightening their burdens, encouraging their hopes, forgiving their sins, and always loving them and leading them closer to God. The Jesus Father Joe was discovering would never use religion or religious law to cut people off from God; nor would He ever do harm to a person's life in order to uphold a law.

For Jesus was the embodiment of God's perfect love for His children, not the embodiment of law; and Jesus attracted people to Him and to His Father's kingdom by the power of that love. Drawn to that love, people wanted to be with Jesus; they wanted to become like Him, and they were willing to follow Him wherever He went. People, quite simply, fell in love with God's absolute and infinite love for them. They, quite simply, fell in love with Jesus.

With this new perception of the man Jesus, Father Joe found that he, too, was falling in love with Jesus all over again; and this new love was bringing him closer to Jesus than he had ever been before. This love was bringing together all the love he had ever felt for Jesus, from the earliest days of his lonely childhood, through his struggles in seminary, to the last pivotal days of his active priesthood. And this love was calling forth in Father Joe an overwhelming desire to spread the "good news," to share his "new sense of Jesus" with others, and to bear witness to the freedom, the healing, and the fulfillment with which he was being graced.

Renewed and propelled by the gifts of his growing intimacy with Jesus, Father Joe waited patiently for guidance, waited faithfully for a vehicle to spread the "good news." And the guidance came; and the vehicle was *Joshua: A Parable for Today.*

Thinking back to those days when he first conceived and gave birth to the Joshua parable, Father Joe recalls: "When I was writing *Joshua*, I felt that God was using me. It was eerie."

~

In 1983, the year that Lech Walesa was awarded the Nobel Peace Prize for his role in leading the Solidarity movement against the Communists in Poland, and some two years after Father Joe had been forced to retire, Joshua came into the world. An answer to Father Joe's most cherished dream – to share his new sense of Jesus with others – Joshua reflected the good shepherd who had inspired his priesthood, the steady, straightforward, and compassionate nature of the man Jesus who had revealed Himself to Father Joe in the pages of the Gospels, and the living, dynamic Jesus who had changed the course of human history.

Set in a small, conservative town in the years directly following Vatican Council II, the Joshua parable provided a background for expressing many of Father Joe's concerns: concerns about the many people whose lives were shattered by the rigid application of religious law; concerns about the increasing fragmentation of the Christian community; concerns about the loss of joy and freedom in people's relationship with God.

The world first meets Joshua, a woodcarver by trade and a newcomer to the small town of Salem, when he comes into the village to buy food:

He wasn't particularly shy, though he didn't talk much. He just went about his business and smiled "hello" to whomever he met along the way. He dressed simply, wearing khaki pants and a plain, loose, pull-over shirt which was a lighter shade brown than the pants. The shirt was tucked in at the waist and open at the neck, which gave a casual, carefree air. In place of a leather belt, he wore a belt put together from carefully braided strings which formed a flat rope about an inch and a half wide, with a loop and large knots which hooked together in the front. The color matched the pants and looked neat, if not dressy.

In appearance Joshua looked tall because he was slim and athletic. His long, graceful hands were used to hard work and were pleasing to watch when he gestured. His face was thin but with strong, rugged features. His blue-green eyes were striking in the deep feeling they expressed. When he looked at you, you had the feeling he was looking into your soul. But the look was not critical. It was filled with compassion and seemed to say, "I know all about you and I understand." His walnut-colored hair was thick and wavy, not long, but not recently cut, so it gathered about his ears and neck.[19]

As the parable unfolds, it becomes increasingly clear that Joshua's thoughts and actions parallel those of Jesus, as if Jesus had just walked into a small town one day as Joshua walked into Salem. Accepting and receiving everyone in the same open, calm manner, responding to their fear and their pain with healing love, and performing quiet miracles of faith, Joshua brings alive the gentle and powerful beauty of the man Jesus. And like the good shepherd, Joshua is ultimately misunderstood and persecuted for his teachings by the more conservative, legalistic elements of the religious hierarchy.

Despite the reforms of Vatican Council II, despite the two millennia that had passed, despite all our innovative technology, history seemed to be repeating itself in Salem; and modern religious leaders appeared to be just as inflexible in the defense of the law as the Pharisees had been during the time of Jesus.

~

In the years that followed the publication of *Joshua*, Father Joe traveled around the country introducing people to Joshua and talking with them about his new sense of Jesus. The reception to his message was slow at first, but within two years, orders for *Joshua* were flooding into Father Joe's small Richelieu Court Publications, and requests for him to speak were rapidly filling up his calendar. Joshua's message of universal love had struck a chord in the hearts of people of every denomination; and Jews, Hindus, Muslims, and Christians, alike, were falling in love with the compassionate, good-natured, ecumenical Joshua. A

Hindu swami wrote to say that he was encouraging his followers to embrace Joshua's teachings; and a Jewish rabbi praised *Joshua* as his favorite book. After the Gulf War, General H. Norman Schwarzkopf, the allied commander of Operation Desert Storm, wrote to Father Joe: "I read your book entirely in two days late at night when I was deeply in need of spiritual strength. *Joshua* brought that strength to me and has given me great peace of mind."

Presented in a modern setting, Joshua, the good shepherd, was capturing the imagination and renewing the faith of hundreds of thousands of people who dreamed of a world unified and healed by God's perfect love. And Joshua and his message were real for these people. They opened shelters for the homeless and named the shelters after Joshua; they organized ecumenical prayer groups in their communities and discussed Joshua's ideas; and faced with a moral dilemma, they asked themselves, "What would Joshua do?"

Although Father Joe had expected that people would like Joshua, he could not have imagined how deeply Joshua would affect those who met him and how real he would become for them. Soon invitations for Father Joe to speak were coming from as far away as Europe and Australia; and the fan mail that arrived at his desk each day was growing into unmanageable mounds: testimonials to the impact Joshua was having on people's lives and on their faith; testimonials to the healing power of the Joshua story; and countless requests, from clergy and laity alike, to meet Father Joe, to visit him, and to spend time with him on retreat.

Father Joe's Joshua ministry was growing quickly; and to accommodate the visitors and retreatants that came from far and wide to meet him, he purchased, with the receipts from the

Joshua sales, a large, old Victorian house with a stately porch high on a hill in Altamont, New York. From the porch, people could see clear across the valley to Albany and Schenectady; and in the small town of Altamont, they could get a sense of life in a town very similar to Salem. Filled with the sound of wind chimes and birds fluttering around delicately hung feeders, the Joshua retreat house was a fitting spot for those who came to meet Father Joe, to renew their faith in an eternally compassionate Jesus, and to nourish their hopes for a world united in God's love.

By 1986, the Macmillan Publishing Company approached Father Joe for the rights to publish a paperback version of *Joshua*. Delighted at the opportunity for *Joshua* to be even more widely distributed, Father Joe agreed to suspend sales of the original Richelieu Court edition so that Macmillan could have exclusive rights to the market for two years. The receipts from the Macmillan sales were barely enough to keep the Joshua retreat house going, but Father Joe had learned, firsthand, that God always found a way to meet his needs. And, besides, the important thing was that the Joshua message was being disseminated far and wide, so far and wide, in fact, that it would eventually be translated into several foreign languages, including Korean and Chinese.

In between talks and retreats, Father Joe began writing his next parable, *Joshua and the Children.* "If Joshua was able to heal so many people when placed in a fictional setting like Salem," he reasoned to himself, "why not place Joshua in a real setting that needed healing, a setting like Northern Ireland." Published in 1989, the same year that the Berlin Wall came down, the book remained on the New York Times Best Seller list for months, followed in 1990 with *The Shepherd,* a novel that finds Joshua inside the Church, preaching about God's universal love to Catholics, Protestants, Muslims, and Jews. In *The Shepherd*, Father Joe addressed his concerns about the gift of celibacy and the diminishing numbers of young men who were entering the priesthood, and about divorce and the growing numbers of divorced people who were being denied the sacraments.

In 1992, the publication of *Joshua in the Holy Land* placed the good shepherd in the Middle East, retracing a path that is two thousand years old in order to bring a final and lasting peace to the region. And in 1995, in *Joshua and the City*, Joshua brings hope and healing love into the most devastated corners of an American urban ghetto, as he faces the overwhelming challenges of poverty, racism, drugs, violence, AIDS, and Satanism.

For the next decade, Father Joe continued to write about Joshua. In *Joshua: The Homecoming,* published in 1999, Joshua addresses many of the concerns facing a world on the brink of a new millennium and attempts to calm their fears. In *The Parables of Joshua,* published in 2001, Joshua uses modern parables to confront difficult contemporary conflicts: the environment, violence in the media, and the admission of female and married priests to the Catholic Church. In the same year, the original *Joshua* was adapted to a screenplay by Brad Mirman and Keith Giglio, and Crusader Entertainment LLC produced the movie. It was directed by Joseph Purdy, with Tony Goldwyn playing the title role.

In *Joshua in a Troubled World,* published in 2005, Joshua addresses the challenges of bringing peace into a post-9/11 world. In the most recent Joshua book, *Joshua's Family,* published in 2007, Father Joe introduces the reader to Joshua's mother and father and the friends and neighbors of his childhood.

In each of the Joshua stories, Joshua faces opposition

from those who fear change and from those who seek to maintain control over other people's thoughts and over the political hierarchy of the day. And in each of the Joshua stories, a fundamental question is implied: "Faced with the political and ethical dilemmas of the modern world, what would Jesus do?"

~

It was now more than twenty-five years since that fateful day when his doctor had told him to retire, twenty-five years he could never have imagined in his most incredible dreams, twenty-five years that had changed his life beyond anything he could have foreseen. At the Joshua House in Altamont, New York, where Father Joe works, the United States Postal Service changed the street address of the Joshua House from Leesome Lane to Joshua Lane; and often, pilgrims from all over the country "drop in," sometimes unexpectedly, to meet Father Joe and receive spiritual direction. Others arrive to take part in scheduled retreats and gatherings at the Joshua House both in Altamont and in Lothian, Maryland, where the Joshua Foundation opened a second retreat house.

In those twenty-five years, Father Joe also continued writing books about Jesus, about the Trinity, and about spirituality and faith. In *Never Alone,* published in 1995, he recounted his companionship with Jesus; in *What Is God?,* published the next year, he shares his experience of God in everyday life. Subsequent books include: *Joey, An Inspiring True Story of Faith; A Portrait of Jesus; Jesus, His Life and Teachings; The Messenger; Trinity, A New Living Spirituality; My Struggle with Faith;* and *The Wisdom of His Compassion: Meditations on the Words and Actions of Jesus,* nominated as the 2009 February Selection by the Catholic Book Club. Father Joe's most recent book, *Jesus, A New Understanding of God's Son,* also published in 2009, is his most comprehensive exploration of Jesus' life, His personality, and His mission – a personality and a mission that is clearly echoed in all the Joshua books.

Father Joe's health has improved somewhat in the years since he was forced to retire from his position as a parish priest, but his doctor continues to monitor his condition, continually cautioning him to slow down, watch his intake of cholesterol and fat, and take his medicine. He listens, as always, with respect, to the doctor; and, as always, he knows that it is God who keeps him alive, not his medicine, not his diet, not even his attempts to find rest in between book tours, retreats, and speaking engagements.

During these years, as he continued to watch Joshua's love touch the lives of so many people with so many vastly different backgrounds, Father Joe slowly began to sense just why God had kept him alive, what God had been preparing him for, and how God had used his steadfast faith and unyielding commitment to Jesus to serve His children. He began to sense that, throughout his life, from the day of his conception, he was being prepared by a merciful and loving God to bring Joshua into a fragmented, wounded world, a world often fragmented and wounded further by those religious leaders whose rigid adherence to the law cut people off from the blessings of an intimate friendship with God.

Looking back over the Joshua years, and over a lifetime filled with so many small and wonderful miracles, Father Joe remains deeply humbled. For his faith journey has led him closer to Jesus, closer to God, and closer to his own unique ministry than he could have ever hoped for. It has led him to meet people from all over the world and from all walks of life and to share with those people the new sense of Jesus that had renewed his own soul and brought him unimagined freedom and joy. And he was graced with the opportunity to see people of every nationality and religious persuasion respond to God's universal love, respond to the healing compassion of the good shepherd and to the living spirit of Jesus among them.

Indeed, his journey with his deeply rooted, living faith had led him to Joshua and to his own spiritual rebirth as The Joshua Priest.

Endnotes

[1] Caryll Houselander, <u>A Rocking Horse Catholic</u> (Westminster, MD: Christian Classics, 1988), 57-58.

[2] Thomas T. Shipley, <u>The Origins of English Words</u> (Baltimore, MD: The Johns Hopkins University Press, 1984), 31.

[3] Joseph F. Girzone, <u>Never Alone</u> (New York: Doubleday, 1994), 4.

[4] Somerset Maugham, <u>Of Human Bondage</u> (NY: Doubleday, 1936), 39.

[5] Maugham, 39.

[6] Maugham, 39.

[7] Girzone, <u>Never Alone</u>, 100-101.

[8] Joseph F. Girzone, <u>Who Will Teach Me?</u> (Rockford, IL: TEL Publishers, 1989), 24-25.

[9] Shipley, 287.

[10] Charles Péguy, <u>The Mystery of the Holy Innocents and Other Poems</u> (New York: Harper, 1956), 27.

[11] Girzone, <u>Never Alone</u>, 34.

[12] Girzone, <u>Never Alone</u>, 34.

[13] Girzone, <u>Never Alone</u>, 22-23.

[14] Shipley, 327.

[15] Girzone, <u>Who Will Teach Me?</u>, 20-21.

[16] Christopher Lasch, <u>The Culture of Narcissism</u> (New York: W.W. Norton & Co., 1979), 2.

[17] Thomas Merton, <u>Conjectures of a Guilty Bystander</u> (New York: Doubleday & Company, 1966), 73.

[18] Holy Father John Paul II, <u>Holy Mass On Boston Common: Homily of His Holiness John Paul II</u> (Vatican: Libreria Editrice Vaticana, 1979), 2.

[19] Joseph F. Girzone, <u>Joshua</u> (Slingerlands, NY: Richelieu Court Publications, 1983), 2-3.

References

Donald Senior, et al., eds. <u>The Catholic Study Bible</u> (New York: Oxford University Press, 1990).

About the Author

An educator, consultant, executive mentor, international retreat leader, and author, Barbara Benjamin is the founding director of Intuitive Discovery, Inc. In that capacity she designs and facilitates programs in leadership, human resources, innovation, and creative and spiritual development for Fortune 500 companies, non-profit organizations, and universities.

Ms. Benjamin has also designed, coproduced, and codirected a sixteen-hour live video program in leadership for the National Technological University. In addition, she has designed and directed a graduate distance learning program in leadership for the School of Business at Mercy College, where she was also an Assistant Professor and mentor. Her speaking engagements include The Writer's Workshop in Geneva, Switzerland, and The Cenacle Center in Houston, Texas. In 1998, Ms. Benjamin codirected The Third Millennium Leadership Assembly in Campobello, New Brunswick, Canada.

Face to Face, Ms. Benjamin's most recent volume of mystical poetry, was nominated for a Pulitzer Prize in 2009. Her first volume of poetry, *Through My Window*, was published in 1988. Her poetry has also been published in *The Connecticut River Review* and *The Fairfield County Catholic* and has been featured in *Celebrate Your Divinity* and *Le Preuve Scientifique de l'Existence de Dieu* by Orest Bedrij.

Ms. Benjamin's other publications include *Leadership in the Interactive Age: A Skills Development Workbook* and the accompanying CDs, *The Leadership Lecture Series; The Case Study: Storytelling in the Industrial Age and Beyond;* and *A Modern Prayer Guide to St. Teresa of Avila's* "Interior Castle." She has also coauthored two cookbooks, *The Lenten Kitchen* and *The Advent Kitchen*, published by The Paulist Press.